The Treasury
under Mrs Thatcher

LEO PLIATZKY

Basil Blackwell

Copyright © Leo Pliatzky 1989

First published 1989

Basil Blackwell Ltd
108 Cowley Road, Oxford, OX4 1JF, UK

Basil Blackwell Inc.
432 Park Avenue South, Suite 1503
New York, NY 10016, USA

British Library Cataloguing in Publication Data

Pliatzky, Leo
  The Treasury under Mrs. Thatcher.
  1. Great Britain. Public expenditure.
  Policies of government
  I. Title
  336.3′9′0941

  ISBN 0–631–16297–6

Library of Congress Cataloging in Publication Data

Pliatzky, Leo.
  The treasury under Mrs. Thatcher / Leo Pliatzky.
    p. cm.
  Includes index.
  ISBN 0–631–16297–6
  1. Government spending policy—Great Britain. 2. Great Britain—
  Appropriations and expenditures. 3. Fiscal policy—Great Britain.
4. Privatization—Great Britain. I. Title.
  HJ7764.P55 1989
  339.5′22′0941—dc19   88–7736

Typeset in 11½/13½pt Bembo
by Witwell Ltd, Southport
Printed in Great Britain

Suave, mari magno turbantibus aequora ventis,
e terra magnum alterius spectare laborem –
non quia vexari quemquamst iucunda voluptas,
sed quibus ipse malis careas quia cernere suave est.

How glad you are, as the winds churn up the waters out on the great sea,
to look on from dry land at another's mighty labours –
not because you take delight in someone else's troubles,
but because you are glad to see what misfortunes you yourself are spared.

Lucretius, De rerum natura

Contents

Acknowledgements

I should like to thank a number of old friends and colleagues who have advised and commented on various aspects of this book, and a number of bodies, including several embassies and High Commissions, who have responded to particular enquiries. I should also like to be able to thank some devoted assistant for relieving me of the secretarial chores, but alas there is no such person.

1

The Treasury and its Ministers

This book is about the Treasury and Treasury policies since Margaret Thatcher became Prime Minister and First Lord of the Treasury in 1979. The latter title means that she is head of the Board of seven Commissioners of Her Majesty's Treasury; the Chancellor of the Exchequer is the Second Lord and the five Junior Lords are Members of Parliament who act as assistants to the Government Chief Whip.

However, like the Board of Trade, it is a phantom Board. In his book *The Treasury*, which appeared in 1964, Lord Bridges wrote: 'Constitutionally the Treasury is governed by a Board of Commissioners who carry out the duties of the ancient office of Lord High Treasurer. The Treasurer's Office has been continuously in commission since 1714; but no meeting of the Board for the transaction of ordinary Treasury business has been held for over 100 years now.' To date, the last meeting of the Treasury Board took place, according to the Treasury, on the occasion of the retirement of the then Permanent Secretary, Sir Douglas Wass, in 1983.

In the past, the Prime Minister did not always hold the post of First Lord of the Treasury, but Lord Salisbury was the last Prime Minister not to do so. The two posts have gone together since 1902. Bridges wrote that, 'It seems unlikely that the two posts will be held separately again since, under the Ministers of the Crown Act, 1937, the payment of a pension to a retired Prime Minister is conditional upon his having held the offices of Prime Minister and First Lord of the Treasury.'

In the more remote past, the position of First Lord, whether or not held by the Prime Minister, appears to have carried with it direct suzerainty over Treasury affairs, but that has long ceased to be the case. The Chancellor of the Exchequer is the minister in charge of the Treasury just as much as the various Secretaries of State and other ministers with Departmental portfolios are in charge of their Departments. Since 1961 the Chancellor of the day has had the support of another senior Treasury minister, the Chief Secretary, who is mainly concerned with public expenditure, and who nowadays has a seat in the Cabinet as a matter of course, though in the past this was not always the case. Traditionally the Treasury has two other ministers – the Financial Secretary, who has historic functions in Parliamentary financial procedures, and the Economic Secretary. The post of Paymaster General has sometimes been used, as is the case now, to provide a fifth Treasury minister.

On the other hand, an interventionist Prime Minister can involve himself in any area of policy that interests him, and even a less interventionist Prime Minister would find it difficult to disinterest himself in such an important area of government business as financial and economic policy. Some have managed to do so, up to a point, in the past, and most Prime Ministers have involved themselves as much or more in foreign policy, which may seem more fun and presents greater opportunities for foreign travel. However, since Britain joined the European Economic Community, the periodic meetings of Heads of Government of the Community countries have required Prime Ministers to involve themselves in economic and foreign policy alike. The further series of meetings of Heads of Government of the world's major non-Communist countries, including the United States of America, has had a similar effect. This suits Margaret Thatcher's natural bent. She can display a remarkably detailed grasp of Treasury matters, and also appears to attach some significance to her titular position and its historical association with Treasury affairs. She once declared in the House of Commons that 'I am proud to be First Lord of it', i.e. of the Treasury. Thus Treasury policies have engaged her interest and have had her active backing, without which they could not have been pursued.

The Treasury, as a 'central Department', has a special place in Whitehall. In contrast with large operational Departments such as, for instance, the Ministry of Defence, which run major services in a relatively – though not altogether – self-contained area of policy, the Treasury is small in numbers but has a wide range of functions relating to the economy and the government machine as a whole. This combination of functions has its critics, on the grounds that not all these responsibilities go well together or that between them they give the Treasury too much power. Some of the critics see the dead hand of the Treasury as an obstacle to expansionist economic policies and would like to loosen the financial brakes. Several recent Prime Ministers shared this suspicion of a strong Treasury, and at various stages some of the Treasury's functions were diluted or transferred to other bodies, as described in more detail a little later on.

However, nearly all these changes have since been reversed. With one notable exception, the wheel has now, meaning 1988, come full circle to where it was when I went to the Treasury in the grade of Principal in 1950. Now, as then, the Treasury plans or controls or coordinates the expenditure, manpower, pay, gradings and management systems of all government Departments and various other public bodies; it has co-ordinating functions for the affairs of the nationalised industries, although it is to the various 'sponsor Departments' that the Boards of those industries report in the first instance; and it has sole Departmental responsibility for macro-economic policy, the Budget and the nation's financial affairs.

In dealing with this wide range of work the Chancellor has at his service not only the Treasury but also two other major Exchequer Departments – Inland Revenue which deals with direct taxes such as income tax and corporation tax, and Customs and Excise dealing with indirect taxes such as import duties, the duties on alcohol and tobacco and Value Added Tax. The Treasury puts together the Budget as a whole and has an important input into taxation policy, including the balance between the various taxes; but it is the two Revenue Departments, as they are jointly known, which have the detailed expertise on each of the taxes and which administer the tax system and carry out the collection of tax payments. The Board of Inland Revenue and the Board of Customs and Excise, consisting of top officials of each Department, have by tradition and statute a great deal of independence in administration and in the treatment of individual cases under the tax laws, as distinct from taxation policy. The administrative load is heavy and, unlike the Treasury, the two Revenue Departments have large staffs and a network of offices round the country.

The Chancellor and the Treasury also rely heavily on the Bank of England, which presides over the banking system as a whole, manages the nation's currency, administers the government's funds and accounts, domestic and external, and advises the government on financial affairs generally and financial markets in particular. The Bank of England does not have the constitutional independence of the Bundesbank in the Federal Republic of Germany or the Federal Reserve Board in the United States. In fact the Bank is owned by the government, since its shares were acquired by Mr Attlee's government as part of its post-war programme of nationalisation, in reaction against the Bank's pre-war reputation for restrictive policies and autocratic disposition. Notwithstanding the current vogue for privatisation, there has been no move to reverse that measure.

Relations between the Treasury and the Bank are normally close but can sometimes be sensitive. If it is to be effective as financial adviser, and retain credibility with the central banks of other major countries – something which can be to the government's own advantage in maintaining the nation's creditworthiness – the Bank has to avoid the appearance of excessive subservience to the government. An effective Governor of the Bank of England has to strike a careful balance between independence of judgement and the Bank's role as an instrument of government policies. But no Governor of the Bank of England would nowadays aspire to the independence of the Bundesbank.

In most other Western countries of which I know, the functions carried out by the Treasury in Britain are divided between at least two Departments. In some cases the broad division is between finance and the budget on the one hand and economic affairs on the other. In the Federal Republic of Germany, for instance, the Ministry of Finance is responsible for both the revenue and expenditure sides of the budget, including the control of central government spending programmes – but not those of the lände – and there is also a separate Ministry of Economic Affairs.

In other cases, economic and financial policy, including the budget, are grouped together, as they are in Britain, but the control of expenditure and staff numbers is split off. This is the case in Australia, for instance, where the Treasury has the former functions but, since 1976, a separate Department of Finance has the latter role. This is also the pattern in Canada, though the name Department of Finance there carries with it the former of these sets of functions, including the budget, while the control of staff and expenditure comes under the Treasury Board, which is in form a Cabinet committee set up by statute.

It is difficult to make comparisons with the United States because of the Presidential system and the division of powers between the President and Congress. The United States Treasury therefore has to co-exist not merely with other executive bodies but also with Congress, which has powers, for instance, to pass budget resolutions setting targets for revenue and expenditure, while Congressional committees have the function of recommending on specific appropriations and revenue measures. Congress also has a large body of staff to serve it in carrying out these functions. In Britain, Parliament and its committees have nothing like these powers and resources. To the extent that comparisons can be made, one could say that the United States Treasury, the Office of Management and Budget, the Office of Personnel Management and the Council of Economic Advisers all have part of the functions carried out in Britain by the Treasury.

In contrast, France is one country where the Ministry of Finance has a span as wide as that of the British Treasury, and in fact a good deal wider. It is composed of a number of Directorates, of which the Treasury is one, which are co-ordinated, on behalf of the Minister of Finance, by the office, or 'cabinet', of a Minister of State. Its title, which has always recognised the Ministry's responsibility for economic policy as well as the usual financial functions, also recognised its role in privatisation during the period of cohabitation after March 1980 between a socialist President and a right-wing Prime Minister, when its full title was 'Ministère de l'Économie, des Finances et de la Privatisation'. This would also be an accurate designation of the British Treasury at the present time.

Financial control appears to be much more centralised in the French than in the British system. For instance, the Ministry of Finance has Inspecteurs des Finances outposted in all spending ministries and municipalities. The Ministry of Finance is also responsible for the audit of all public expenditure, whereas in Britain the finances of central government Departments and certain other public bodies are now audited by the National Audit Office, which in 1983 succeeded the Exchequer and Audit Department and was transferred from Treasury oversight to the direct control of the Public Accounts Committee of the House of Commons. The audit of local authority finances in Britain now comes within the purview of a body called the Audit Commission. In this particular matter I feel sure that we should not copy the French audit arrangements, which have in the past been criticised as cumbersome and slow moving. In general, however, the Inspecteurs des Finances are an elite corps and the reputation of the Ministry of Finance stands high.

Thus there are a number of ways of organising these central functions of government. All of them, if we leave aside the special case of the United States, appear to work. Up to a point, good civil servants, such as are to be found in all these countries, can make almost any administrative system work, but no doubt some require more effort than others. The separation of expenditure control from the rest of the finance function in Australia and Canada requires close collaboration between the two Departments involved in each of those countries. I would see no gain, and a good deal of disadvantage, in making a similar split in Britain, as was at one stage contemplated during James Callaghan's premiership. Although the decision went against that particular change – but not before the Treasury had gone through some anxious moments while the issue was in doubt –

over time there have been a number of moves to curtail the Treasury's influence. Let me enumerate them.

A split, on the German pattern, took place at the outset of Harold Wilson's first administration – as I have narrated elsewhere – when the Department of Economic Affairs was set up with the object of providing 'creative tension' *vis-à-vis* the Treasury. That was an idea which worked very badly, partly but not solely because of the erratic character of the Department's first Secretary of State. A hastily drawn up concordat to lay down demarcation rules failed to resolve the underlying problems of overlapping functions and duplication of responsibilities, as well as the problem of political rivalry. The Chancellor of the Exchequer, James Callaghan, who was later to become Prime Minister, had the effective levers of economic management, including fiscal and monetary policy, but had to expend a great deal of time and energy in clearing his lines with George Brown in order to use them. The principal call made on the time of the first Permanent Secretary of the new Department was handling the relationship with the Treasury and helping to smoothe the troubled waters. The DEA was wound up after George Brown had been succeeded by politically less weighty ministers, and James Callaghan was succeeded at the Treasury by Roy Jenkins, who was in a position to resist any encroachment on his powers as Chancellor.

A further split took place under Harold Wilson, when the Civil Service Department was hived off from the Treasury in 1968. This went part way, as it were, towards the Australian or Canadian model; that is to say, the Civil Service Department had the oversight of staff numbers, pay and other personnel matters, but the Treasury remained responsible for public expenditure generally as well as for economic and budgetary policy.

The demarcation issues presented by the formation of the Civil Service Department were not, initially at any rate, anything like as intractable as in the case of the DEA. Problems were to emerge in the course of time, but the Treasury did not see the Civil Service Department as a rival in its core activities. Large areas of the personnel function were of little concern to Treasury people with a primarily financial or economic bent. I have been criticised for writing that, when the split took place, 'I was relieved not to be at risk any longer of being shifted back to Establishments work as my next posting in the Treasury', on the grounds that this displays the typical contempt of the Treasury mandarin for the management function. But this central function in relation to the rest of the civil service was not management as one knows it in a major operational Department, and still less like management in an industrial company. It was management at a distance, through the medium of Departmental Establishment Officers, with no direct contact with those managed. It was preoccupied with rules rather than people, and tended to be slow-moving and lacking in urgency.

The Civil Service Department survived throughout the Conservative administration of Mr Edward Heath, who succeeded Harold Wilson in 1970, and also throughout the 1974–79 Labour government under Harold Wilson and then James Callaghan; but it was wound up by Margaret Thatcher in 1981. The truncation of the Treasury was then largely reversed. We will return to this in more detail later on.

A further dilution of the Treasury's responsibilities, though one which had little more than nuisance value, took place when the Central Policy Review Staff was set up within the Cabinet Office during Edward Heath's premiership. The remit of the CPRS went much wider than public expenditure, but it had two particular functions in that field. One was to prepare a paper on public expenditure priorities, jointly with the Treasury, for circulation to Cabinet at the beginning of each annual public expenditure exercise. The other was to share with the Treasury the co-ordination of Departmental Programme Analysis and Reviews – PAR for short. Although the CPRS lived on during the Wilson – Callaghan era, the Treasury left it to its own devices in the preparation of its papers on priorities, which had no discernible practical effect, and the PAR reviews, which had not been a success, were discontinued.

The CPRS was retained by Margaret Thatcher for a time but was wound up in 1983. Its decease, hastened by some embarrassing leaks of work in hand on one or two sensitive issues, is still mourned by some, such as Tessa (later Baroness)

Blackstone and William Plowden, later Director of the Royal Institute of Public Administration, who served in the CPRS at one time, and who believe that there is a role for a body without Departmental bias to brief Cabinet as a whole on the pros and cons of the available options. There are some others who are in a position to judge and who believe that there is now a gap in that respect. Perhaps if the CPRS in its early days had not been given a specific remit in a Treasury field such as public expenditure, without having the expertise for the job, I might have taken a more charitable view of the concept. Those recruited to the CPRS, whether from within Whitehall or from outside, undoubtedly found a certain appeal in their relatively freebooting role in operating at the centre, and in breaking new ground. The pioneers of the Department of Economic Affairs also mourned the passing of that Department, for somewhat similar reasons; some of them used to meet every year in a public house to keep its memory green.

A more serious infringement of the responsibilities of the Chancellor of the Exchequer – then Anthony Barber – and the Treasury took place when Edward Heath, finding the Treasury not expansionist enough for his liking, put William Armstrong in charge of masterminding his economic U-turn. This exercise, which I have described elsewhere in more detail, led, among other things, to the interventionist Industry Act of 1972. Armstrong had by then moved from the Post of Permanent Secretary to the Treasury to become the first Permanent Secretary of the Civil Service Department, and had initially thrown himself into the work of setting it up. However, after the first flush of creation had worn off, he was ready to answer the call to return to the economic arena. While retaining his post as the head of the Civil Service Department – which, as a Department, was in no way involved in this special exercise – he operated for a time over part of the Treaury's field of interest. However, this was an *ad hoc* arrangement and did not leave any continuing institutional set-up behind it.

The Policy Unit in No. 10 Downing Street was a new body which had its birth during Harold Wilson's second term of office and was kept in being by James Callaghan and Margaret

Thatcher in turn. Under Mrs Thatcher, the role of the Policy Unit developed as that of the CPRS waned and was finally extinguished. Unlike the CPRS, the Policy Unit's role is to provide the Prime Minister, and not Cabinet as a whole, with ideas and advice alternative or supplementary to those flowing from the regular Whitehall policy machine. For instance, while the Cabinet Office secretariat provide the Prime Minister with a largely procedural steering brief for meetings of Cabinet or Cabinet committees, Mrs Thatcher has also had a separate note from the Policy Unit on points arising from Departmental policy proposals under consideration.

Critics of Mrs Thatcher's allegedly over-dominant style of government, including a number of former members of her Cabinet whose services were not retained, point to the build-up of her staff in No. 10 as evidence of a drift towards Presidential as opposed to Cabinet government. However, John Hoskyns, later Director General of the Institute of Directors, who was her first head of the No. 10 Policy Unit, seems to have experienced some disappointment at its limitations. The total number of policy advisers in the unit, plus other special advisers who have been recruited to the Prime Minister's office – such as Alan Walters, who was her high-level economic adviser for a time – in conjunction with the little band of Private Secretaries, have never numbered more than fifteen to twenty, which is tiny compared to the staff of the White House in Washington, and small, I believe, by comparison with, say, the Prime Minister's office in Australia, and probably the staffs of many other Western Heads of Government. If Margaret Thatcher has stamped herself on her times, it is not because of the size of her immediate entourage.

In addition to the Policy Unit, Margaret Thatcher has from time to time appointed particular individuals either as advisers in a chosen field – Alan Walters as economic adviser has already been mentioned – or to carry out special assignments. The outstanding example is Derek Rayner, who was borrowed from Marks and Spencer to mastermind the 'Rayner scrutinies' of various services, and subsequently returned to Marks and Spencer to become its Chairman. The work which he started has been developed and carried on by the Efficiency Unit, reporting direct to the Prime Minister. Anyone operating under the Prime Minister's authority can carry a certain amount of clout in Whitehall, as I found in a much more limited role when carrying out a review of 'quangos' in 1979. However, no one working for Margaret Thatcher as Prime Minister seems to me to have fulfilled the role of guru or *eminence grise* to the same extent as Horace Wilson did for Neville Chamberlain or Professor Lindeman did for Winston Churchill.

I have heard it suggested by one close observer of the scene that the size of the Prime Minister's entourage cannot go beyond a certain point because of the limited office space in No. 10, notwithstanding the surprising warren of accommodation which lies behind the relatively modest frontage of Downing Street. It is true that pockets of staff can report to the Prime Minister without being located in No. 10 but, if advisers are to be involved in the day-to-day flow of paper and business of government, there is nothing like being on the spot or, like the Secretary of the Cabinet, a short distance away through a connecting door. (The Chancellor of the Exchequer also has access through a connecting door from No. 11 Downing Street.) Bernard (later Lord) Donoughue, the first head of the Policy Unit under Harold Wilson and James Callaghan, and Alan Walters both attached importance to being in No. 10. On this approach, the time to worry about our going over to a Presidential system will be when a British Prime Minister decides to build a White House or an Élysée Palace.

However, I doubt whether it is really enlightening to pursue the comparison with a Presidential system. The institutional differences between the British and the American systems of government remain as wide as ever. What is supposed to have changed under Margaret Thatcher? Her penchant for doing business in Cabinet committees or in *ad hoc* ministerial groups, rather than in full Cabinet, is well known; but, though this may have gone further than under her predecessors, they too handled some sensitive matters in Cabinet committees and kept them away from full Cabinet as long as possible. Mrs Thatcher has used the power of appointment and dismissal so as to secure, over time, a Cabinet which has suited her, but Harold Macmillan showed greater ruthlessness when a whole batch of Cabinet ministers were despatched in the night of the long knives in July 1962. If Harold Wilson and James Callaghan preserved more of a balance between the different wings of the Labour Party, not merely in Cabinet but within the ministerial teams in individual Departments, that was their preferred way of seeking to hold a naturally fissiparous party together.

Margaret Thatcher has, however, had a single-minded view of the purposes for which she has wished to use office, and her appointments and dismissals have been designed to produce a reasonably like-minded Cabinet. One observer has commented that the Cabinet system has remained intact but that she has operated it so as to get her way. If analogies are useful at all, a somewhat better analogy might be drawn with a 'hands-on' chairman and chief executive of a very large corporation, with a hand-picked Board of Directors. Her position has been progressively strengthened by winning three general elections, and by her durability as Prime Minister, in contrast to Harold Macmillan who handed over the Premiership because of ill health, though he subsequently remained a public figure for many years, or Edward Heath who called and lost a general election when faced with a miners' strike, Harold Wilson who had simply had enough and handed over at the age of sixty, and James Callaghan who lost whatever chance he had of re-election by not going to the country in October 1978 and was then undermined by the winter of discontent. Most of these Prime Ministers, and perhaps all of them, could have held on to office longer if they had chosen to act differently. It is arguable that, so long as she gets her way in Cabinet and has a majority in Parliament, where no Conservative Prime Minister in modern times has been voted out by his supporters – even Chamberlain had a majority of eighty in the crucial vote on his conduct of the war in 1940, though he subsequently resigned to make way for a coalition government – she has had more power within the country than President Reagan has had in the United States, though Britain, unlike the United States, is no longer a major force in the world.

How has all this affected the Treasury? It does not seem to me that such limited build-up as has taken place in the Prime Minister's entourage adds up to a duplication or dilution of the Treasury's role such as the Department of Economic Affairs, or the Civil Service Department, or the CPRS, or William Armstrong's role in the U-turn, or Harold Lever's roving commission as financial wizard under Wilson and Callaghan, in their different ways were meant to bring about. Margaret Thatcher has wanted to have her own advisers, including the Policy Unit and the Efficiency Unit, which have sometimes been a nuisance to the Treasury, but the restoration to the Treasury of most of its old functions suggests that she has also wanted a strong Treasury capable of delivering the policies which she supports. Although in one sense No. 10 is at the very centre of government in Britain, in terms of the allocation of functions the Treasury and the Cabinet Office are now once again the only two fully fledged central Departments in Whitehall.

The Chancellor has not always got his way with the Prime Minister – witness the position on the European Monetary System – but I should have said that she has backed him in the general thrust of his financial strategy and has, as a result, enabled him largely to get his way within the government as a whole. This made it all the more surprising when a public airing of differences on interest rates took place before the 1988 Budget, to which we will return near the end of the book.

2

The Head of the Civil Service

In one respect the wheel had not come full circle by the date of this book to the situation when I went to the Treasury in 1950. The Permanent Secretary to the Treasury at that time, Sir Edward Bridges, was also Head of the Civil Service. The formal introduction of this title followed a reorganisation of the Treasury in September 1919, when according to Henry Roseveare's book, *The Treasury*, a Treasury Circular on 15 September 1919 'informed the Departments that he [the Permanent Secretary to the Treasury] was to "act as Permanent Head of the Civil Service and advise the First Lord in regard to Civil Service appointments and decorations."' More than one distinguished former Permanent Secretary has told me that this was the work of a famous Permanent Secretary to the Treasury, Sir Warren Fisher, but he did not arrive in the Treasury to take up that post until October 1919 and, although he had had some input into the reorganisation, Roseveare writes that it 'cannot be assumed that "he got himself designated Head of the Civil Service."' Then, as now, the allocation of this title was surrounded by controversy.

From 1956 two changes took place. The post was redesignated Head of the Home Civil Service, as a concession to the claims of the Foreign Office. And from that date there were joint Permanent Secretaries to the Treasury, one of whom held this title. A further change took place when the title passed to the first Permanent Secretary of the newly created Civil Service Department, Sir William Armstrong, who later became Lord Armstrong of Sanderstead but is now deceased. The title was inherited by his successors at the CSD, Sir Douglas Allen (later Lord Croham) and then Sir Ian Bancroft (later Lord Bancroft). Then came a complex series of changes, which I summarise only for the sake of completeness. It is the end result which is of interest and a matter of some controversy.

First, the Prime Minister's dissatisfaction with the Civil Service Department as an instrument for managing the service came to a head over the handling of pay disputes in the civil service, and the Department was disbanded. Lord Soames, the Minister responsible, under the Prime Minister, for the Civil Service Department lost his place in Cabinet. Bancroft's retirement was brought forward somewhat; after a short interval, he received a life peerage.

Some of the former functions of the Civil Service Department, especially control of civil service pay and numbers, returned to the Treasury. Others were retained in a truncated body with the title of Management and Personnel Office. This body had a Second Permanent Secretary as its immediate head, who came under the Secretary of the Cabinet, Sir Robert Armstrong, and it was in effect a sub-Department of the Cabinet Office. Responsibility for the Financial Management Initiative, which will be discussed later in the book, was shared between the MPO and the Treasury. The title and functions of Head of the Home Civil Service were shared by Armstrong and the Permanent Secretary to the Treasury, Sir Douglas Wass. When the latter retired in the normal course in 1983, Robert Armstrong became the sole Head of the Home Civil Service.

This division of labour in the personnel field was evidently not felt to be working well; perhaps the Treasury felt that it did not have all the levers it needed for its control functions. In October 1987 the Management and Personnel Office in its turn ceased to exist; its Second Permanent Secretary and some of its other staff and functions, including its share in responsibility for the FMI, were transferred to the Treasury. However, the handling of the most senior public service appointments, and certain other personnel questions such as the conduct of the civil service and issues concerning the structure of government, remained in the Office of the Minister for the Civil Service within the Cabinet

Office. The OMCS also retained responsibility for the Civil Service Commission, which handles the recruitment of civil servants, and for the Civil Service College. Robert Armstrong continued as Head of the Home Civil Service and, on his retirement, his successor as Secretary of the Cabinet, Sir Robin Butler, succeeded to that title.

The end result, therefore, of this history of events is that the Secretary of the Cabinet has become Head of the Home Civil Service ex officio, as it were, though not necessarily for ever. The Secretary of the Cabinet is in one aspect a servant of Cabinet as a whole, with responsibility for the functioning of the Cabinet Office machine and the organisation of the numerous ministerial Cabinet Committees and the various interdepartmental committees of officials which meet in the Cabinet Office and come under its aegis. (There are many more official committees which are not Cabinet Office committees.) In another aspect the Secretary of the Cabinet has a special role as aide and adviser to the Prime Minister. In addition, he has particular responsibilities under the Prime Minister, for intelligence and security matters. When the further role of Head of the Home Civil Service is added, and especially his role in top-level appointments, the influence of his position is clearly very great indeed.

Spokesmen of civil service trade unions, and others with an interest in constitutional matters, have voiced strong criticisms of the decision to combine the post of Head of the Home Civil Service with that of Secretary of the Cabinet. The two functions, it is argued, are different, even conflicting. One man cannot combine the heavy workload of the Secretary of the Cabinet with responsibility for the morale, standards and conditions of hundreds of thousands of servants of the state. He is bound to short-change this latter responsibility. There are some who see the civil service as a counterpart to the fighting services, holding allegiance ultimately to the Crown and requiring its own head, as a separate appointment, to preserve the integrity of the service and its non-party-political character.

A frequently cited example of the shortcomings of the new arrangement is the *cause célèbre* of Government Communications

Headquarters, a crucial intelligence-gathering establishment, whose staff, in the interests of state security and to avoid jeopardising intelligence links with the United States, had their right to belong to a trade union removed from them. Since the decision to do this was taken by the Prime Minister, and since the Head of the Home Civil Service, her principal adviser on such matters, was also, as Secretary of the Cabinet, there to serve the Prime Minister, it is argued that there was no one within government to speak for the interests and viewpoint of the GCHQ civil servants.

If we assume for the time being that there should be such a post as Head of the Civil Service, or of the Home Civil Service, where else would it be better located? There are some strong arguments against its being returned to the Treasury. The Permanent Secretary to the Treasury already has a great deal on his plate. He would be even worse placed for such activities as getting round the country and visiting civil service establishments – something for which the Secretary of the Cabinet does in fact seek to find time. Moreover, if you are looking for someone who would identify with the interests of the civil servants and side with them – as some commentators seem to expect the Head of the Home Civil Service to do, though I think it is a misconception – in some respects the Treasury is the last place to look. In pay disputes, in particular, it is bound to be on the other side. When I first went there, Treasury officials were known for their hair-shirt attitudes, making it a point of honour to seek to deny themselves, along with everyone else, the benefits in which they would share if they conceded claims by the civil service unions.

If it were proposed to bring back the Civil Service Department, with the intention that its Permanent Secretary could be a, so to speak, more free-standing Head of the Civil Service, that would also bring back the ambivalence which played a part in the demise of the CSD. To the extent that it identified with the interests of the civil service, or was thought to do so, it sowed the seeds of its own dissolution. The Department could in fact claim that it delivered whatever staff cuts were set by governments from time to time. Nevertheless, whether justly or not, it was suspected of not having its heart in the drive for economy in civil service pay and staff costs.

The notion of the Head of the Civil Service as in some sense a representative of its interests seems to me a fairly recent development and far removed from the main purpose underlying the original introduction of the title, which was to assert the Treasury's hegemony and central role *vis-à-vis* other Departments. If the idea is taken so far as to imply that the holder of the post should be champion of a specific civil service point of view in all aspects of civil service affairs, to the point if necessary of standing up for that point of view against the Prime Minister, that seems to me something of a mirage, probably at any time and certainly under the present regime.

I do not mean to imply that a non-party-political civil service, with its own ethos and traditions which should be upheld, is a mirage. I am inclined to think that the concept of allegiance to the Crown contributes something to the continuity of the service through changes in government, but I do not see how, in any situation which I have experienced, officials can serve the Crown otherwise than through the elected government of the day. Certainly civil servants should not be required to commit any illegality – and I am not aware of any case in which that has occurred – or any impropriety. The couple of recent *causes célèbres* in which that has been an issue have been most exceptional: it should be the responsibility of Departmental Permanent Secretaries and not merely the Head of the Civil Service to protect civil servants from any improper pressures, but in practice most civil servants go through the whole of their careers without encountering problems of this kind. Having one's advice ignored or overruled is a more common experience and one of the hazards of the profession; less senior officials suffer this treatment at the hands of more senior officials more commonly than at the hands of ministers, with whom they may not have much contact.

The interests and point of view of management and of those managed will in many matters not be identical in the civil service any more than in other organisations. In such matters, especially the matter of pay, it is for the civil service trade unions to represent their members. Certainly the Treasury and the employing Departments should behave as good employers; in this, as in other fields, senior officials should be capable of taking account of representations made to them and giving ministers balanced advice. (There is no reason to assume that they failed to do so in the GCHQ affair.) But in matters of money an identity of interest and viewpoint is not the norm. A Head of the Civil Service who would somehow identify himself with both sides and both interests is hardly feasible.

In other countries there are certain civil service matters relating, broadly, to standards and conduct, responsibility for which is located elsewhere than in the Department controlling budgets and civil service costs. The range of such matters is wider in some cases than in others. In France the Ministère de la Fonction Publique et des Réformes Administratifs has this role; the work is shared by two junior ministers under the Prime Minister. In the Federal Republic of Germany something of the same role is performed by the Ministry of the Interior. In neither case is there a top official with the title of Head of the Civil Service or with a central role in recommending senior appointments.

In Australia personnel matters of this kind come under neither the Treasury nor the Department of Finance but under the Head of the Office of the Prime Minister and the Cabinet; and in Canada they come under the Clerk of the Privy Council and Secretary of the Cabinet. These posts approximate somewhat more closely to that of Head of the Civil Service, but neither carries that title. Nor is there any such position in the United States.

After the winding up of the Civil Service Department it must have been an open question whether the title of Head of the Home Civil Service should be perpetuated. The Secretary of the Cabinet could have taken on responsibility for non-Treasury aspects of the service without carrying that additional title. He is well placed for that purpose, in particular for advising on senior appointments, because of his frequent (almost daily) access to the Prime Minister. The Permanent Secretary to the Civil Service Department had been at a disadvantage through not having a similar ease of access: this is one of the factors which had made that a less important and satisfactory job than it may sound.

On the other hand, the title has by now acquired a certain patina. It has no doubt enhanced the status of the Secretary of the Cabinet in such matters as promulgating a statement of the duties and responsibilities of civil servants, and in providing a figure to whom civil servants with problems of conscience can, in the last resort, appeal. It is always interesting to see how things are done or not done in other countries, but we do not always have to do the same. A certain feeling which already exists in the civil service that it is held in less esteem than in the past might well have been aggravated if the separate post of Head of the Home Civil Service had been dropped, and this might well have attracted more criticism than combining it with the post of Secretary of the Cabinet. The balance of argument appears therefore to lie with retention of the post, provided that there are no unrealistic expectations of it.

3

Questions of Strategy

Treasury policies under Margaret Thatcher and her two Chancellors of the Exchequer, Geoffrey Howe followed by Nigel Lawson, have been enshrined in the Medium Term Financial Strategy. The formulation of this strategy is generally credited to Nigel Lawson, who at that time was Financial Secretary to the Treasury. This is a ministerial post of much longer standing historically than that of Chief Secretary to the Treasury (which was created in 1961 to relieve the pressure on the Chancellor on the public expenditure front), but of less seniority in the ministerial pecking order. However, Nigel Lawson had more influence on overall Treasury policies than most recent Financial Secretaries. Other members of the Treasury circle, according to William Keegan in his book *Mrs Thatcher's Economic Experiment*, had mooted the idea of a medium-term plan to reduce inflation, but by all accounts it was Lawson who gave it impetus.

The MTFS was promulgated at the time of the Budget in March 1980, but the underlying concepts were brought into the Treasury by the new team of ministers and their special advisers from the moment the new government took office in 1979, and displaced overnight the previously prevailing concepts of Keynesian demand management and whatever was left of the commitment to full employment.

The ultimate objectives of the strategy were a reduction in the rate of growth of the quantity of money and, through that, a reduction in the rate of inflation. There is already some tendency to forget how alarming inflation had become at that time and how large it loomed in the concerns of the new government. Other elements in the strategy were reductions in public expenditure, taxation and public borrowing. Fiscal policy, which brings expenditure and taxation together in the Budget, along with government borrowing to bridge any gap between the two, is a straightforward concept, though there can of course be disagreements about what the policy should be. But monetary policy is a much less accessible subject. We will therefore put further discussion of the subject off for the time being. However, it should be said at this stage that, though practically everything else in the MTFS went off course, Treasury ministers have stuck through thick and thin to the progressive reduction of public borrowing – even when unemployment, at its peak, rose to roughly ten times the level of twenty years earlier, and neo-Keynesian doctrine would have indicated a more expansionist Budget – and, whatever the connection, inflation did eventually come down.

One of the things which went off course was public expenditure. Planned cuts turned into large increases, and the government has now settled for a moderate continuing increase in the *absolute* amount, while seeking to reduce public expenditure as a *proportion* of national income. In contrast, privatisation of publicly owned industries, or denationalisation as it used to be called, has gone farther and faster than was ever planned at the outset, and the receipts from these special sales of assets have helped significantly in reducing the need for public borrowing. In conjunction with sales of council houses to their tenants, this programme has greatly increased the number of people owning at least some property – their own home, or a few shares, or both – and has contributed to a shift in popular attitudes towards public and private ownership.

There need be no suprise that things turned out differently from expectations, since that is a common experience for governments, especially new governments. It is also easy to explain why they turned out differently in these two fields of policy. Industries such as telecommunications or airlines or gas and electricity supply, whether they are in the public or the private sector from the point of view of ownership, are in the *market* sector of the economy. Some of them have a sheltered market, with a greater or lesser degree of monopoly, but they are all supplying tradeable goods and services, at a price, to meet a market requirement. Though governments sometimes have them run at a loss, they are capable of making a profit. They are thus capable of being transferred from public to private ownership, if the circumstances are right for it: we will discuss later on why they have been right in the 1980s.

On the other hand, the free or subsidised public services, such as the state schools or the National Health Service, are taken out of the market. They are not run on a commercial basis and do not make profits. They could not be privatised without changing their whole character. The customers of British Telecom will not have noticed a change in the whole character of the service since privatisation. The phone bills still come in; it is still hard, but perhaps no harder, to find a telephone kiosk in working order in a city area. But parents would notice a change in the character of the education system if all the state schools became private schools overnight and started to charge fees, as the independent schools already do.

To say that a public service is 'taken out of the market' means that the character of the service and the amount spent on it are determined by government, central or local, not by the profit which the supplier can make and the price which the customer will pay out of his own pocket. It does not mean that there cannot be at least a quasi-market element in the arrangements or that the public authorities must do everything in-house and by direct labour. The army, for instance, consists of direct labour, so to speak, but the uniforms and rations are bought in on a commercial basis, not manufactured by the Ministry of Defence. Cleaning and laundering in hospitals can be contracted out to companies which put in the most competitive bid. Whole services, such as refuse collection, can be contracted out by local authorities.

In my view it can without doubt be salutary that an alternative to in-house provision and direct labour should be available, but the choice should be a matter of which option works best and not of ideology. In industry also there is frequently a choice to be made between providing a service in-house or contracting it out, and the balance of considerations does not always go the same way. But the essential question in the present context is not which method of supplying the service should be adopted, but whether the very existence and the whole character of the service should or should not be determined purely by the market.

If cleaning and laundering are contracted out in hospitals, costs may or may not be cut, and patients may or may not notice a change in the cleanliness of the sheets and the lino floors, but the existence of the hospital, and its financing, still remain outside the market, and the character of the health service is in that sense different from the character of the private sector of medicine. But the whole character of the service would be changed, and patients would certainly notice the difference, if all the hospitals and the family doctor service went on to a commercial fee-paying regime. It must be doubtful whether most of the people who were happy to buy a few shares in British Telecom or British Gas would be happy – though some few of them might be – to see such a change in the health service, or whether they have been happy at the apparent deterioration in the service. This illustrates why cutting public expenditure has been more difficult than privatisation.

There is increased acceptance today, even in previously unlikely places such as the Kremlin and Labour Party Headquarters, of the advantages of the market economy as a system for allocating resources in response to customer choice and for decentralising economic decisions. But probably few people are so doctrinaire as to deny that some services cannot or should not be left to the market, or so philistine as to believe that the market by itself would provide a society which was not only secure from external attack and internal disorder, but also reasonably disease-free and adequately educated, and in which the edge would be taken off the most acute poverty.

All Western countries have a substantial non-market sector, larger in some than in others, or – if the term is preferred – a high level of public services. All of them, therefore, and especially those with a relatively large non-market sector, have to resolve a number of difficult questions:

1 Which services should be taken out of the market?
2 How much should be spent on the public services in total?
3 How are priorities to be decided – how to determine the amount to be allowed for each service, when government decision has been substituted for market forces and there is nothing equivalent to consumer demand and the profit motive to resolve the choices which have to be made?
4 How can efficiency and value for money be secured in the management of non-market services when the disciplines of competition and profit and loss do not operate?

In the following chapters let us see what answers have been given to these questions under this Conservative government, though it may be convenient to take them in a different order.

4

The Return of Realism

To the question 'How much?', the Conservative government's first answer was that public expenditure should be frozen. Its second answer was that it should be cut. But neither freeze nor cuts took place. The total rose inexorably each year.

That is to say, a White Paper in November 1979, which was in the nature of a holding operation, stated that 'the Government's economic strategy must be to stabilise public spending for the time being.' In March 1980 a further White Paper announced that: 'The Government intend to reduce public expenditure in volume terms over the next four years.' But in fact from 1978–79 to 1984–85, inclusive, total public expenditure rose by roughly 11 per cent on one of the definitions in current White Papers, and by about 14 per cent on another of the definitions. Because of the inflation which was raging in the earlier part of this period, the cash total approximately doubled, on either definition.

Some of the reasons why things did not go according to plan were more predictable than others. To start with, the new government simply had too many commitments. In 1979 it took over its predecessor's undertaking in NATO to increase defence spending by 3 per cent a year in real terms, and also its plans for increased spending on the health service. These are two of the four biggest public expenditure programmes. Education is another of these four, but a large part of this expenditure is in the hands of local authorities, and the government proved unable to cut it, or to prevent recurring excesses in local authority expenditure as a whole, in spite of a series of new curbs imposed on local government.

In addition, there was a large increase in the cost of social security, which is by far the biggest programme of all, because of the steep rise in the number of unemployed drawing benefit. Thus, the Treasury was powerless to make cuts or prevent increases in the four programmes which, at the start of the first term accounted for over 60 per cent of spending by central government Departments and local authorities, a figure which is now over 70 per cent. A high priority was also given to spending on the police. All these increases were more than could be offset by cuts, some of them severe, in the remaining programmes.

Finally, we must mention the costs of dealing with the two most dramatic events in this period, the Falklands war in the government's first term of office, and the miners' strike in the second. The latter added about £2 billion to expenditure in 1984–85, but the outcome removed for the foreseeable future the previously recurrent threat to bring down the government of the day by industrial action and must have played a significant part in the change which took place in the industrial climate.

In 1984 the Treasury again floated the idea of freezing public expenditure, and at this attempt, after a time-lag, it came closer to success. This strategy was canvassed in a Green Paper on Public Expenditure and Taxation into the 1990s, issued in March 1984, which argued that all the extra resources from economic growth would have to be applied to tax reductions if the recent upward trend in taxation was to be reversed. (So-called Green Papers are a form of consultative document which has been in use since 1967; White Papers, which go back much further, are policy documents, and have been used since the late 1960s for annual statements of public expenditure plans.) The freeze did not take straight away, but over the three years 1984–85 to 1987–88 public expenditure in real terms was virtually unchanged on one of the definitions now used in White Papers – the Planning Total, as it is called, which takes credit for privatisation proceeds as negative expenditure; another of the totals used (general government expenditure, *excluding* privatisation proceeds) rose only 2.5 per cent over these three years. (The Treasury itself does not like to take 1984–85 as the starting point for such comparisons, because expenditure in that year was inflated by the costs of the miners' strike, but even if we allow for this the growth of expenditure was slowing down in this latter phase.)

We now come to the latest target, which has looked like being comfortably achieved; the declared aim has been to reduce public spending as a proportion of GDP, that is the Gross Domestic Product which, in its various versions, can be used as a measure of the nation's income or expenditure or output. (Anyone familiar with economic and financial statistics will know that there are different definitions or versions of many of the important aggregates; any reader new to this field will now be discovering this fact of life.) A reduction in the ratio of expenditure to GDP was in fact already taking place, but under the new dispensation a moderate rise in expenditure was accepted so long as it was less than the growth of GDP. Thus, the January 1988 public expenditure White Paper states that 'The plans for government spending should allow growth in real terms of about 1½ per cent a year, well below the expected growth of national income.'

Both of these new approaches – stabilisation or, even more so, limited growth – were more realistic than the Draconian but abortive plans of the first five years. For one thing, they started from a higher level, in which many of the pressures for more spending had already been accommodated. Then, the NATO undertaking ran out in 1985–86, and there was even some reduction in the defence budget in the following year, instead of the previous annual increases. In addition, the rise in the number of unemployed on benefit slowed down during this phase and even took a downward dip. There were measures to contain the cost of social security as a whole by a policy intended to target benefits on the most needy, while reducing the value of universal child benefit in real terms. The social security bill did in fact level out for a while towards the end of this phase.

Meanwhile this somewhat more relaxed policy stance – if the Treasury can ever be said to be even relatively relaxed – had become politically more acceptable to the government's own supporters. The radical right, as it is sometimes called, had been critical of the failure to cut expenditure in the earlier years, while public borrowing was high, but their criticisms were blunted by the subsequent fall in the borrowing figures. Privatisation helped, both by contributing to the fall in borrowing, and by rolling back the frontiers of the state through an alternative route.

Some of the pressures for public spending were in fact now coming from the other wing of the government's own supporters. The approach of the 1987 general election may have given some added force to these concerns. Electoral considerations do not, in my view, play as pervasive a role in government decisions as is sometimes believed. There are many issues presenting dilemmas and conflicts of considerations which thoughts of the next election do nothing to resolve, while I do not imagine that such thoughts animated the government in any way in decisions on the handling of such matters as the Falklands war and the miners' strike. Nevertheless, the approach of an election must have some effect on the political climate in which decisions are taken. At any rate, both the public expenditure White Paper of January 1987 and that of January 1988 stated that, as compared with the last White Paper, extra funds had been allocated to the government's priority services, including health, education and law and order, while the estimated costs of the demand-led social security programme had also risen. The 1988 White Paper also listed the inner cities as a priority programme, and a further addition arose from acknowledging the excess in local authority spending.

There emerges from these developments an impression of a Treasury which is increasingly realistic, and which is given increased room for manoeuvre by the state of the economy, and which is increasingly in control, though holding down a number of bottled up pressures, especially in the health service. Having a government which – after the previous alternation of different parties in office – won three successive terms of office made a great deal of difference to this progression. The annual rate of increase in total spending (general government expenditure excluding privatisation proceeds) declined from 2.2 per cent in real terms in the four financial years which corresponded roughly to the first of these terms of office (1978–79 to 1982–83) to 1.6 per cent in the next four years, (1982–83 to 1986–87) to a projected rate of 1.3 per cent for the period 1986–87 to 1990–91. There was actually a fall in this total of 0.5 per cent in real terms in 1987–88.

As is illustrated by the history of these years, the question how much in total to allocate to the public services cannot be answered in the abstract. We have to start from where we are and decide in which direction we want to move. It is useful to have a strategy which gives a perspective of more than a year at a time, but it is usually a mistake to get hooked on detailed plans too firmly and for too far ahead, and one has to be prepared to adjust the strategy as one goes along.

A strategy which relates public expenditure to GDP makes good sense, in my view, though the concept has its critics. That part of public expenditure which consists of the supply of goods and services, such as schools and teachers, hospitals and doctors, contributes to GDP (just as private schools and doctors in private practice do) as well as constituting a charge on it. The remaining part consists of transfer payments, such as social security or subsidies to farmers or payments of debt interest to holders of government securities. This indirect government expenditure, as it is sometimes called, is a charge on GDP but contributes and adds nothing to it. It is sometimes argued that it does not make sense to lump together, in the same formula, the former (direct) type of expenditure, which features in both the numerator and the denominator of the public expenditure/GDP arithmetic, and transfer payments, which are an element in the numerator only. It is also sometimes argued that transfer payments 'only' redistribute income, and that, in considering how much public expenditure the nation can afford, we should be concerned only with those services, such as defence or health or education, which directly utilise physical resources of manpower and materials.

On the other hand, the public expenditure total covering both types of programme is a measure of the amount which has to be raised by revenue and by public borrowing. It is also an approximate indication of the demands made by public expenditure on the output of the economy. These two factors –

the requirement for taxation and borrowing and the constraints of available output – are highly relevant in answering the question of what the total of public expenditure should be.

It can be better understood that this is not solely a budgetary problem but also a resource problem if we think in terms of the market sector on the one hand (including any publicly owned trading enterprises) and the non-market sector on the other. As a simple illustration, let us assume a very underdeveloped country in which the market sector consists of peasants producing rice, bananas, and such-like products for their own consumption or for sale, and the non-market sector consists of soldiers, providing defence, law and order, and government generally. The number of soldiers that the country can keep is limited by the amount of rice, bananas etc. which the peasants produce and the proportion of it which can be taxed away from them, or simply appropriated for the use of the soldiers.

This particular illustration comes from a paper I prepared for the Asian Development Bank. More complex versions (featuring car workers, social workers and pensioners instead of peasants and soldiers) appeared in my book *Paying and Choosing*; this developed the concepts of the market and non-market sectors quite independently of a conceptually identical approach in an earlier book called *Britain's Economic Problem: Too Few Producers* by two well-known Oxford economists, Robert Bacon and Walter Eltis. (In some other respects there are substantial differences in the scope of my book and theirs, which has a great deal more mathematical backing.)

The point is that only the market sector satisfies the demand for tradeable goods and services. The size of the non-market sector – that is, the free or subsidised public services – is governed by two things. These are first the markets sector's output of tradeable goods and services, and second the proportion of that output which the government is willing and able to extract by taxation or public borrowing.

There are a number of important points which are common to the Bacon and Eltis thesis and mine. First, the distinction between the market and non-market sectors is not a matter of private and public ownership. Publicly owned industries are in the market sector to the extent that they operate by selling tradeable goods and services, while privately owned industries such as agriculture, as well as loss-making publicly owned industries, are taken out of the market to the extent that they rely on subsidies. They are hybrid creatures. Second, public expenditure on transfer payments makes demands, indirectly, on the market sector just as much as public expenditure on goods and services does. Social security payments, for instance, finance demands by pensioners, etc which can be satisfied only by the supply of tradeable goods and services. In a phrase from Bacon and Eltis, ' ... all the money that workers, salary earners and pensioners spend must necessarily go to buy marketed output.' Finally, these are not value judgements; to quote Bacon and Eltis again, ' ... almost all the civilised activities of a modern society are wholly or largely non-marketed. Both Covent Garden and Glyndebourne cover only a fraction of their costs by selling tickets ... '. The question is how much of the economy can be in the Covent Garden and Glyndebourne category.

The public expenditure:GDP ratio is not the same thing as the ratio of the non-market sector to the market sector, but the two will move in the same direction. Changes in the public expenditure:GDP ratio are therefore a good indication of whether more or less is being taken out of the market economy for public spending, and consequently whether more or less is being left for other purposes – private consumption, industrial investment and exports.

The public expenditure White Paper has graphs to show the government's progress in reducing the public expenditure:GDP ratio. One line in the graphs shows the figures of general government expenditure in which privatisation proceeds are netted off so as to reduce the total; another line shows these figures *excluding* privatisation proceeds. I am glad to say that the Treasury now give primacy to the latter figures. On this basis the ratio has come down from 46.25 per cent in 1984–85 to 42.5 per cent in 1987–88, and is projected gradually to fall further in the next few years. So the Treasury has no need to cook the books in order to show that the objective is being achieved.

It can sometimes be a moot point whether receipts should be

netted off in the expenditure side of public accounts or shown on the revenue side. If, for instance, a Department regularly buys or sells land and buildings in the ordinary course of its activities, as several of them do, it may be sensible to net off the proceeds. But the special sales of assets since 1979 are so untypical and on such a large scale as to justify presentation as an extraordinary item which has helped to finance expenditure rather than to reduce it. It is the difference between cutting household expenditure and paying for it by selling off the family silver, to quote the late Lord Stockton, formerly Harold Macmillan.

I have therefore only one quibble with the line of figures which excludes these special receipts. Although the 1988 White Paper refers to 'general government expenditure, which is the combined spending of central and local government including debt interest and is a comprehensive measure of the amount which has to be raised by taxation and borrowing', the figures of gross debt interest overstate by £5 billion to £6 billion a year the amount which has to be financed by taxation or borrowing, since there is a flow of automatic interest receipts which should be netted off. These receipts have been running at roughly a third of the gross figure. Moreover there has been a significant double-counting of debt interest on public housing and the subsidies paid towards it. It is the burden of deadweight national debt which has to be financed out of taxation and borrowing, not the gross debt interest figures: on this basis, the public expenditure total would be reduced by several percentage points. However, the point is purely presentational and, so long as the error is reasonably constant, it does not affect the trend in the public expenditure:GDP ratio.

It is sometimes argued that a strategy for public expenditure which is expressed in terms of this ratio is flawed, because it cannot hold good in a recession when economic growth slows down or turns negative; the probable effect of cutting planned expenditure in order to match the new and lower profile for GDP would be to worsen the recession and aggravate the problem of under-used resources.

In the post-1979 slump the government did not see the issue in those terms. It was not a question of pursuing or modifying its own chosen spending strategy, but of seeking to establish a different overall strategy from the policies which it had inherited. Moreover, the problem was not one of a 1930s type slump, with falling prices, but of slumpflation with output and employment falling but pay and prices rising. Reducing inflation, therefore, had an overriding priority, not maintaining employment.

The strategy which has now emerged – that is, reducing expenditure as a proportion of GDP – has still to stand the test of time, and in particular it has not so far been put to the test of a fresh recession. It is impossible to foresee in detail what the circumstances of a future recession might be, or what recasting of policies might be called for; for instance, the balance of payments may be an increasingly serious complication in any future conjuncture. But the mere existence of the present public expenditure strategy would surely not dictate an attempt to reduce expenditure in the short term in line with a temporary downward kink in the projections of economic growth.

On the contrary, as happened in both the 1930s and the early 1980s, in the short term one would expect both the cost of unemployment benefits and the public expenditure:GDP ratio to rise in a future recession. That need not invalidate the longer term objective of gearing the trend in expenditure to the trend in GDP. Meanwhile, so long as economic growth continues, there is room for continuing argument about the precise division of the spoils.

5

The Public Expenditure System –
the Rules of the Game

The machinery for allocating money to the various public services is the annual Public Expenditure Survey. This is the instrument for implementing the public expenditure strategy and it is the framework for the final determination of priorities.

In Whitehall it used to be frequently referred to as the PESC system, after the Public Expenditure Survey Committee which co-ordinates the Survey. The particular method in use is described as cash planning. What else, it might be asked, would the Treasury plan, if not cash? The answer is that it used to plan 'volumes', which brings us to the question – what prices do you plan in? This can be rephrased as – what allowance is made for inflation in the plan? This may sound a dry technical issue, until it comes down to concrete cases such as increases in nurses' pay – should the Treasury 'fund' the increases? – at which point the issue becomes quite emotive. This crucial issue will be discussed separately a little later on.

The evolution of the system was described in my book *Getting and Spending*. Things have moved on, and in this book I will deal with the system as it is now, in 1988, not how it got here, apart from the special question of the price basis of planning. Some things, however, remain constant, including the magnitude of the exercise, with general government expenditure now running at over £180 billion – one hundred and eighty thousand million pounds or £180,000,000,000 – a year and expected to rise to £200 billion in the next two years. The volume of paper and data to be processed is as vast as ever. Each annual exercise occupies the better part of the year, and the struggle for the Treasury is unremitting. Under a government ideologically opposed to high state spending, it might be imagined that the Treasury would not be under the same age-old pressure from spending Departments, but in practice, though the Treasury may not have its back to the wall in quite the same way as at some times in the past, life on the public expenditure front appears to remain quite stressful.

The Public Expenditure Survey Committee consists of Principal Finance Officers from spending Departments, with a senior Treasury official in the chair, but it can only do the ground work for ministers. The term 'PESC system' is misleading if it gives the impression that the crucial decisions are taken by officials, and this particular piece of shorthand is now rather outdated. The intermediate processes are technocratic, but the key decisions are political. The ground rules are approved by Cabinet at the start of each year's exercise, and Cabinet approves the results which are published at the end in the Autumn Statment and in the annual Public Expenditure White Paper. There are proposals to rationalise these two documents, which now overlap a good deal, but up to 1988 the White Paper has remained the key work of reference.

In the White Paper, the total amount allocated to spending Departments is broken down by Departments (or groups of Departments) for each of which there is a separate chapter, or two chapters for a couple of the big spenders, fleshing out the bare bones of the summary breakdown with detailed description and analysis. Scotland, Wales and Northern Ireland each have a separate chapter covering a wide range of services which are administered by the Scottish, Welsh and Northern Ireland Offices respectively, but excluding those services which are administered for the United Kingdom (such as defence) or for Great Britain (such as social security) as a whole.

Over the years the White Paper has been expanded and developed out of all recognition compared with the initial White Papers extemporised in the late 1960s. It has sometimes appeared in a single volume, and sometimes in two, which I in my time preferred. In the 1988 White Paper, which in fact has blue covers, the first volume, analysing public expenditure as a whole, and the second volume containing the individual chapters, between them have over 500 large pages. The presentation has been greatly improved, and the information contained is encyclopaedic.

In addition to the Departmental programmes, there is a sum put to reserve, to be drawn down for new developments in the course of the year. (This used to be called the contingency reserve, but the term was always being confused with the Contingencies Fund, successor to the Civil Contingencies Fund, which is something quite different – an account from which money is temporarily advanced to tide Departments through until Parliament has approved their Estimates in full – and the Treasury now call the arrangement simply 'the reserve'. In this book I will use that term or the term 'public expenditure reserve'. It is not a fund like the Contingencies Fund from which actual money can be obtained; the reserve exists only on paper in the Treasury's books, but allocations from the reserve entitle Departments to get more money.) The Departmental programmes plus the public expenditure reserve but minus privatisation proceeds make up what is called the planning total, within which each year's exercise must be contained.

The planning total differs from the figures of general government expenditure quoted earlier in this chapter, principally because the former total excludes debt interest, which is not deemed to be plannable in the same way as other components of public expenditure. Other and less important differences are the treatment of public corporations and some purely accounting items. It has also been decided to change the treatment of local authority expenditure in the planning total; the change will be explained later in the book.

The Survey system is constantly evolving, partly to meet the requirements of the time, and partly because different generations of officials – and sometimes ministers – have different ideas on how it should be operated. It has no statutory basis and probably no two Surveys are exactly alike, but the general pattern is now as follows.

The Survey covers a four-year period, comprising the

financial year in which the Survey is carried out ('the current year') and three financial years ahead, referred to as Years One, Two and Three. The current year's figures have already been settled in the previous Survey, and in the normal way will not change during the exercise, apart from the transfer of sums from the public expenditure reserve to individual programmes as the year progresses.

The figures for the two years ahead – Year One and Year Two – have also been determined in the last Survey and published in the last Autumn Statement and White Paper, but they are now reviewed and are to that extent not immutable; it is normal for spending Departments to try to get the figures changed in their favour. The White Paper figures provide the baseline, or point of departure, for these two years but Departments can put in additional bids, as they are called, to increase the White Paper figures.

There is a great deal at stake in these bids. For the spending Department they represent their hopes and ambitions – the extra motorway, the new research project, the improvement in welfare schemes, or simply the avoidance of a deterioration in an existing service. For the Treasury they add up to a threat to the overall financial strategy. Its initial posture must therefore be to seek to whittle down the bids or to secure economies in existing programmes to make room for them and also to rebuild the contingency reserve.

A new rule has been introduced in recent years that all additional bids must be tabled by means of a letter at ministerial level to the Chief Secretary; this precludes Principal Finance Officers from putting in bids at official level which their ministers are not prepared to fight for. Claims for additional money may be based on a variety of grounds – new developments since the last White Paper, the inadequacy of the baseline figures for carrying out government policy, evidence that actual inflation has been running above the allowance made for it. Moreover some programmes are open-ended or demand-led, and extra money has to be found if demand is greater than previously estimated. You cannot, for instance, turn away the last man in the dole queue or the last pensioner to present his pension book at the post office on the grounds that there is no more money in the kitty, and you cannot find the money by giving less to all the unemployed and all the pensioners unless ministers are prepared to legislate to cut the rates of benefit. They may in due course make economies in the social security bill as a whole, but that takes time.

In some cases a Department may, between two Survey exercises, have secured an extra allocation for the current year from the public expenditure reserve, on one or other of these grounds. This does not automatically raise the baseline for the Survey and carry through into subsequent years. If the Department seeks to convert its temporary gain into a continuing increase, it has to do so by putting in an additional bid. If the reasons for making the allocation from the reserve in the first place still hold good, there must be some presumption in the Department's favour.

In each successive public expenditure exercise, one old year drops out and one new year comes in. The year which was previously looked forward to as Year One, now becomes 'the current year'. The former Year Two becomes Year One and the former Year Three becomes Year Two. Thus we come to a new Year Three, a *tabula rasa* for which no baseline figures exist to start with. The gap is filled by projecting Departmental programmes forward into the extra year on the basis of a formula for which the Treasury has obtained Cabinet approval as part of the ground rules for the exercise. In principle a variety of different formulas would be possible; the formula actually in use at present is to up-rate the Year Two baseline figures – the latest year for which figures already exist – roughly in line with, or slightly below, the prospective rate of inflation for Year 3 indicated by the current update of the Medium Term Financial Strategy in the Red Book (i.e. the Financial Statement and Budget Report.) Thus the baseline established for the new Year 3 provides for no increase in the programme in real terms. If a Department believes that it has a case for a real increase, its minister must put in an additional bid for the final year of the new Survey.

The onus is thus on the spending Department, as demandeur,

to make its case, and I have no doubt that this is as it should be. Otherwise the Treasury would have a hopeless task in seeking to hold the line, wherever it was drawn. The particular line which the Treasury seeks to hold, under the current strategy, will be as close as possible to the planning totals in the last public expenditure White Paper. For the planning total as a whole, as well as for individual programmes, the old White Paper figures for each Survey year, with only limited adjustments, will provide the baseline for the new exercise; something to this effect will have been agreed in the ground rules for the exercise. However, to start the exercise from an existing baseline is one thing; to end up with the same figures is another. In this government's earlier years, as we have seen, the ideal of rolling plans forward with a reasonable degree of continuity was not achieved; on the contrary, an upward revision of plans took place from one White Paper to another. Even in recent years this tendency has persisted.

Year after year, even with a government whose philosophy is inimical to high spending, additional bids have been reported in the press – always seemingly well informed of the progress of the exercise – which between them, if approved in full, would raise the planning total by some billions. There is always some room for negotiation within existing plans, as the planning total for each future year always includes a large reserve; the further away the year, the larger the reserve allowed for in that year's plans. As the time approaches, part of the reserve can be allocated in advance to meet additional bids, but if too much is given away before the beginning of a financial year there will not be enough left for contingencies and developments during the year.

The negotiations on additional bids have increasingly been taking place at ministerial level. There will normally be a feeling out of positions at official level, but increasingly the contribution of officials has been confined to clarifying the facts and the arguments, so as to clear the way for an appraisal in the Treasury of the extent to which the bids for more money can be accommodated and of the excess which has to be eliminated. A paper is then circulated to Cabinet by the Chief Secretary (with a formal covering note by the Chancellor, in the days when the Chief Secretary himself was not a member of the Cabinet); on the basis of this paper Cabinet approves a total within which efforts must be made to contain the additional bids. This stage is generally reached in July, before Parliament's long summer recess.

In the autumn, when ministers get down to regular work again, a series of 'bilaterals' (as opposed to meetings of ministers collectively) takes place between the Chief Secretary and individual spending ministers. In these bilaterals, some bids are conceded, others may be withdrawn or a compromise may be reached, and others may be unresolved at this stage. As a matter of protocol, the Chancellor does not entertain appeals from spending ministers against positions taken by the Chief Secretary, even though the latter acts under the Chancellor's authority.

The bilaterals have become an increasingly well established event in the political calendar, and a Chief Secretary can acquire a reputation for having done well in the bilaterals, or not so well, as the case may be, though it is not always clear what doing well consists of. Whereas there have been only two Chancellors of the Exchequer, Geoffrey Howe and Nigel Lawson, from the Conservative victory in 1979 to mid-1988, there have been five Chief Secretaries. Curiously, the first three of these, John Biffen and Leon Brittan, who moved up in the government on leaving the Treasury, and Peter Rees who did not but who moved up to the House of Lords, were all out of the government, for one reason or another, by the latter date. John MacGregor was then Minister of Agriculture and John Major was the current Chief Secretary. Curiously again, although Peter Rees did not get a regular place in the government team, he had probably conceded fewest runs of the five in the bilaterals.

In recent years it has been a fairly regular practice to deal with issues which have not been settled in the bilaterals by means of a new machinery introduced during the Margaret Thatcher administration for adjudicating on differences between the Treasury and spending ministers. This is a ministerial committee popularly known as the Star Chamber, after the original Star

Chamber, a court which in Tudor times was responsible for the torture and execution of the king's enemies. Under the present more enlightened regime, the committee's judgements may be a matter of life or death to the ambitions of spending ministers, though not to their persons.

In the past I have heard Whitelaw himself describe what a tense experience it could be to go into the Cabinet room when a memorandum of his was on the agenda, and to know that the future of his policies, perhaps of his political career, depended on his success in putting his proposals over to the colleagues ranged round the Cabinet table. There may be a less formal atmosphere to the Star Chamber than to Cabinet, but the stakes can nevertheless be high. When a conclusion is reached, whether in the bilaterals or in the Star Chamber, and subject to ratification by Cabinet, to increase the spending plans for a particular service, it will then be described, in the Autumn Statement and the White Paper, as one of 'the Government's priority services'. So far as can be made out, the Star Chamber is the nearest this government gets to a collective discussion or determination of priorities.

The Star Chamber is not a continuing Cabinet committee, such as those dealing with, say, home affairs or defence and overseas policy, which meet at intervals throughout the year and go on from government to government, possibly with a change of nomenclature. It is one of quite a large number of *ad hoc* committees which are set up and meet as required, with a serial number rather than a title – for instance, GEN 48 or Misc 55 – and are then stood down. In principle the Star Chamber would not be reconvened if all public expenditure issues could be settled without recourse to it. In practice it was set up regularly each year during Margaret Thatcher's second term of office, under the Chairmanship of William (later Lord) Whitelaw, the Deputy Prime Minister. The ministers who sit on the committee, with a very senior Cabinet Office official as their secretary, are not themselves parties to the dispute. They cannot override the planning total approved by Cabinet; subject to that, they can overrule the Treasury and spending ministers. In principle a minister who is overruled in this way can take his case to full

Cabinet, but it appears that such appeals have been rare and have not achieved significant additions.

The Star Chamber seems to me to have been an important and effective development in the final determination of priorities. The whole process through which priorities become established, from beginning to end, and the influences which play a part, are more complex than that. They range from the works of the great opinion-makers, through the framing of the manifesto, to the drafting of the Queen's Speech, to the Survey system which has just been described. Pressure groups also come into the process. But something like the Star Chamber seems to me an instrument which future governments, of whatever political complexion, should have available.

By all accounts, the success of the Star Chamber in discharging its remit owed a great deal to the authority and standing of William Whitelaw. In 1976, when I explored the idea of a ministerial committee with a somewhat similar role – in the first instance to adjudicate on claims on the contingency reserve – one of the problems raised was the difficulty of finding non-spending ministers of suitable calibre to sit on the committee. Admittedly it will not always be easy to find a Willy Whitelaw figure as chairman. Nevertheless, after Whitelaw's ill health made him unavailable for further service in that role, it was generally assumed that the Star Chamber would be reconvened, if necessary, under a new chairman; in the summer of 1988 it was in fact make known that Mr Cecil Parkinson would become its chairman in the autumn, which was generally taken as a sign of Prime Ministerial favour, since there was no operational need to issue this little bit of news at that stage. A future government which attached sufficient importance to the Star Chamber idea would no doubt find a chairman and members for it.

Let us go back to the public expenditure exercise. When all outstanding issues have been resolved by the processes which have been described, the final results of the exercise go back to Cabinet for approval. Since 1982, the first public announcement of these results has been made in the Autumn Statement, along with the economic forecast which the Treasury is obliged to publish under the Industry Act 1975; the requirement to publish this forecast arose from a clause inserted in that legislation on the initiative of Dr Jeremy Bray, at that time a backbench Labour Member of Parliament. Further details, and the Departmental chapters, have followed in the public expenditure White Paper in the New Year.

A little more will be said in Chapter 8 about the development of the Autumn Statement, which is now destined to displace the White Paper. The debate on the Autumn Statement now provides the first and the principal occasion for discussing the government's spending plans.

The public expenditure Survey system emerges from this description as, at certain crucial stages, a massive framework for negotiations between Treasury ministers and spending ministers. This takes place in the context of the government's general political philosophy and manifesto commitments and also of the particular pressures and problems of the day. I have argued in the past that, while many factors are at work in the processes of decision-making on public expenditure, it is the force of ideas and the force of circumstance which are the most powerful, freqently pushing in different directions. This seems to be still a valid perception, which is borne out by the history of public expenditure under the post-1979 government.

A belief in the market economy and competition and in rolling back the frontiers of the state provide the dominant ideas in the government's economic philosophy. The circumstances which blew the government off course in its initial attempts to apply these ideas to public expenditure were discussed in the last chapter. In any event the government clearly accepts that there are some functions which cannot be left to the market. We can only infer what these are or what the priorities are among them; there are today no dissertations on priorities such as the late CPRS were licensed to produce.

In economic and social theory there are some principles to guide us in deciding what services cannot be left to the market. Two of these, which go back to Adam Smith, though in different terminology, are the concept of public goods, which can be provided and enjoyed only collectively; and the concept of externalities – the divergence between private and social costs and benefits which arises from the external effects (or neighbourhood effects) of what we do, and because of which the market by itself cannot produce an optimum result. To these we should add the concept of the distribution function of the state, at least to take the edge off the worst of poverty and to provide for the special needs of the handicapped and the sick, for which the market will not provide.

At first blush the government's expenditure decisions appear to reflect these principles rather faithfully. The programmes which absorb most money could all be justified by these concepts. The 1988 White Paper states that 'extra resources have been allocated to the Government's priority activities, including health, education, law and order, defence and inner cities.' All of these flow from the concepts of public goods and externalities. Social security is not described as a priority but is in fact the largest programme; the White Paper states, more grudgingly, as a recognition of the force of circumstance, that 'Provision for social security ... has also been increased.'

But the government's preference for market solutions and for competition can be seen in the increased role which it seeks for the private sector, operating wherever possible side by side with the state – in education, health and pensions, for instance – and in reduced dependence on the state by, for example, the universities and the arts. And at the end of the day a certain amount evidently depends, if only at the margin, on the negotiating skills and strengths of individual ministers.

6

Cash Planning

The public expenditure negotiations are complicated by the need to allow for inflation, which is the bugbear of financial planning. From the mid-1970s to the early 1980s, when the rate of inflation in Britain was particularly high by our standards (as opposed to, say, Latin American standards), rising to peaks of over 24 per cent in 1975 and 21 per cent in 1980, the problem of allowing for increases in pay and prices in the public services was severe. The history of that period has coloured the financial policies of Margaret Thatcher's government. The defeat of inflation has been its top priority.

Differential rates of inflation are an added complication. The phenomenon of differential inflation or relative price movements in everyday life has become familiar through the behaviour of house prices in recent years, which have risen more than prices generally and have risen much more in the London area than elsewhere in Britain. Families and businesses have to take account of inflation and make provision for it as best they can – sometimes they may even make a profit out of it – but they cannot do anything to change it. The provision that governments make for inflation may help to change it; at the least it may influence people's expectations about inflation.

To set into perspective how this problem is dealt with now, it will be helpful to recapitulate briefly how it was handled in the past. In the first instance the government has to make provision for inflation in the coming financial year. Until the mid-1970s this was done by presenting Main Estimates to Parliament to obtain its formal approval for Departmental expenditure in the financial year ahead; these were based on pay and prices as they stood just before the beginning of the financial year. Supplementary Estimates were presented later in the year to cover pay and prices increases and any other changes. Everyone concerned with the spending of public money could proceed in the expectation that, if pay and other costs went up, the money would be found for them. This procedure has a long history, ante-dating the Survey system by far, and for a good many years I am not aware that anyone found fault with it. It was the emergence of cost-push inflation which dictated the need for something more.

Before the Survey system was introduced in the 1960s, there was no problem about the treatment of inflation in medium-term spending plans, because there were no such plans. It was the Survey system which brought the problem with it. The solution adopted was that the expenditure projections for future years represented 'volume' programmes at 'constant prices'. In other words, they were index-linked. For instance, if the defence budget was planned to rise by 3 per cent a year in real terms, the White Paper would show defence expenditure going up by 3 per cent each year; no allowance for pay or price increases was calculated in advance but, when the time came, the figures would be scaled up to cover inflation, whether general or differential, and to deliver that volume of 3 per cent extra in terms of manpower, equipment and so on. The object was to allocate real resources rather than money. It was a planning system rather than a control system, and planning was geared to economic growth. The system was not designed to cope with a period of high inflation; when such a period arrived, the system facilitated it and was undermined by it. The method of adjusting to rising pay and prices offered no resistance to general inflationary pressures, and no incentive to economise in or switch from those items of expenditure which were particularly swollen by relative inflation.

In 1976 the Labour government changed the method of providing for the next financial year by introducing cash limits over a wide range of programmes. These put a limit in advance on the cash which would be available for Main Estimates and

Supplementary Estimates combined and thus on the rate of inflation which the Exchequer would be prepared to finance. This measure was seen by Denis Healey and Joel Barnet, the Chancellor and Chief Secretary of the time, as a back-up for their policies to restrain pay and price increases, but it also proved an effective instrument for economy generally. I myself played some part in persuading spending Departments that the will existed to make cash limits stick. Cash limits could not, however, be applied to open-ended programmes, in particular social security benefits, which operate automatically, though in 1988 a limit has been put on one untypical social security programme, the Social Fund, under which payments are not automatic.

At that stage the Survey system as a whole remained largely intact, but the arrangements for cash limits were superimposed on it. The projections still represented volume programmes. No attempt was made to anticipate what the rate of inflation would actually be in the later years of the Survey period. But, when each year came round, the indexation of programmes could not exceed the rate of inflation allowed for in the cash limits which were set at the beginning of the year.

The new ministerial team in 1979 disliked this system. 'All that indexation!' one of them exclaimed. They had a distaste for indexation generally, which they saw as an undesirable mechanism for accommodating inflation rather than as a sometimes necessary protection against its effects. A hankering to de-index civil service pensions was not endorsed by a committee set up to report on the subject. Powers were taken to under-index unemployment benefits, but were used only once, and that economy was reversed the following year. In the case of the public expenditure system, there were practical reasons, and not merely an ideological hostility to indexation, for getting away from constant prices and volume planning; it was a tortuous system and could be a hindrance rather than a help to control. In 1981, urged on by the Prime Minister, who took a close and well informed interest in the intricacies of the subject, the Treasury took the plunge and switched at a stroke from volume planning to cash planning of public expenditure.

Although inflation at the start of the 1981 Survey was running at 13 per cent, programmes for the next three years were calculated in advance on the assumption that prices in those years would rise by 7 per cent, 6 per cent and 5 per cent respectively.

The change of system has succeeded remarkably well in achieving its objectives. One can only speculate what would have happened if inflation had not come down as projected – how far real programmes would have been cut to fit the Procrustean bed of the cash plans, or how far the planning figures would have been stretched to accommodate higher-than-planned cost increases. From the first, the public expenditure reserve has provided a fall-back, from which individual programmes could be topped up if it turned out that the cash plans had under-provided for inflation, but there had to be limits to the reserve itself. In the event, the reduction of inflation took place even more rapidly than planned, so that in one year spending Departments actually had money to spare because of an over-generous allowance for inflation.

In the first flush of change, as so often happens, revolutionary fervour went to excess. Volumes were out; cash, and cash alone, was in. The Treasury's attitude appeared to be that from now on the expenditure dialogue would be conducted only in cash terms, without reference to what the cash would buy. The White Paper figures of past expenditure and projections of future expenditure were presented solely in cash terms, nowhere translated into real terms. If the commentary referred to planned increases in certain programmes, this might be a sort of newspeak for a reduction in real terms. This was a reflection of the ultra-monetarist philosophy, then in its heyday.

Gradually, as the Treasury became more secure in the new way of doing thing, the White Paper reverted to a more meaningful presentation, employing both cash terms and real terms, in the sense of cash adjusted for the general rate of inflation (by means of the GDP deflator) but not adjusted for relative inflation. But the problem of the 'relative price effect', or differential inflation, still exists. It is a problem which is bound to arise when cash planning is applied to pay increases, so long as pay goes up more than prices generally.

As we have seen, under the rules of the game an uplift for inflation in line with the MTFS is the essence of the formula used for rolling programmes forward in the Survey so as to establish figures for the final year of the Survey period, i.e. Year 3. After a couple of years, these figures become the baseline for negotiations about next year's money; for instance, the financial year 1989–90, which was Year 3 in the 1986 exercise, becomes Year 1 in the 1988 exercise, and so on. No doubt many other adjustments will have been made to programmes in the meanwhile, and the original uplift for inflation may be obscured by the passage of time. Nevertheless, to the extent that the baseline makes provision for pay and price increases in the year ahead, it must logically do so on the basis of that earlier projection of the general rate of inflation.

Even if this allowance for general inflation proves to be adequate to cover other cost increases – and it is more likely that the Treasury, out of an occupational preference for lower rather than higher figures, will have pitched it on the mean side, as spending Departments believe – in a 'normal' year it will be unlikely to cover increases in rates of pay. In the economy as a whole, although pay increases in the 1980s have ceased to be geared to double figure inflation, earnings have continued to rise year by year more than the general rate of inflation. This has been largely true of public service pay also, though it has generally lagged behind increases in the private sector. So the pay bill tends to exceed the provision for it which is built into the baseline figures in the public expenditure survey.

This excess can be dealt with in one of three ways. A spending Department can bid in advance, during the Survey negotiations with the Treasury, for an additional amount to cover the foreseeable excess. Or it can seek an extra allocation from the public expenditure reserve after the pay increase has been decided upon. Or it can absorb the excess by economies in its expenditure as a whole. In the civil service, it appears to have been this last course which was generally adopted by Departments in a number of years in the 1980s. In part the money was found by economies in administrative expenditure other than pay; in part, also, the under-funding of civil service pay tended to add an extra squeeze to the contraction of civil service numbers which, up to 1988, was taking place anyway. By running staff numbers down more quickly than was originally planned to their end-of-year targets, Departments were able to release money to pay their remaining staff. This, i.e. a volume reduction, is the right response, according to some theorists, to a relative price increase.

The bulk of public expenditure does not go on the pay of civil servants but on the 'programme expenditure' which they administer. If we look at the four largest programmes, we find that the operation of cash planning affects them in different ways – or not at all in the case of social security, which is the biggest programme of all, running at about £66 billion (excluding the costs of adminstration) in 1988–89, or about 30 per cent of the 'planning total'. The majority of benefits, though not all of them, are up-rated each year in line with increases in the Retail Price Index. Projections of social security expenditure in the later years of the Survey are based on illustrative future changes in the RPI but, when the time comes, benefits are up-rated in line with actual inflation, not the projections. Thus, there is no volume squeeze on benefits, in the sense that on average they maintain their purchasing power, though in relative terms they have not been keeping pace with the rise of living standards enjoyed by most of those in employment.

Nor had cash planning in itself anything to do with the furore in 1988 over changes in the rates of benefit which made some people a little better off and many others worse off. These changes resulted from a policy review in which it was decided to target benefits on certain categories of the needy. Since the review appears to have been constrained by an approximate ceiling on total benefits to existing claimants, other needy groups were bound to lose. The prospect that the total social security bill will nevertheless rise again appears to be due to an increased uptake of benefits.

Let us move on to the National Health Service which, by 1987, appeared to be in crisis because of shortage of money, while at the same time more money was being spent on the service than ever before. In 1988–89 the NHS accounts for over £17.5 billion out of some £20.5 billion to be spent on the health and personal social services programme, as it is called. 'Gross spending on the NHS has risen by an estimated 32 per cent in real terms between 1978–79 and 1987–88,' claimed the White Paper.

How is this paradox of poverty in spite of such plenty to be explained? The problem with these figures is that an increase 'in real terms' means after allowing for the general rate of inflation, whereas the NHS has, over a period of years, experienced 'in service' inflation at a much higher rate, because of increases in pay and other costs. It is in the matter of current costs (as distinct from capital expenditure) in the hospital and community health services that the resulting squeeze has been most felt; the family practitioner service has fared distinctly better. Estimates for the five years up to 1986–87 suggest that differential inflation in the former services left almost no increase in purchasing power. The slender margin for service development came almost entirely from 'cost improvements' achieved through higher efficiency in the use of resources.

Even so, the money provided should have been more than enough if the demands on the health service had been static, but in fact it had to cope with a variety of new or growing demands – the very old, drug abuse, AIDS and new treatments which create their own waiting lists. There has been an extra squeeze on London hospitals because of the policy of redistributing resources to other regions which are held not to have been getting their fair share. London apart, on one view the crisis has been largely confined to expensive hi-tech treatments, such as hole in the heart surgery on babies, and to 'elective' medicine, such as hip replacements.

In recent years the health service has had recurrent moments of suspense while waiting to find out whether the government would 'fund' the latest pay increases in full or would require part of the cost to be absorbed by economies in the service. It will be recalled that, in the Spring of 1988, this developed into high drama as the public waited on, first, the recommendations of the review board on nurses' pay, and then on the government's decision on finding the extra money required. Some undisclosed provision had been made for this requirement, but something more than a parsimonious award was indicated by the critical shortage of trained nurses, and it was generally and rightly assumed that a substantial topping up of the existing provision would be needed. Well informed reports that, against the background of alleged crisis in the service and widespread public sympathy for the nurses, ministers were reconciled in advance to fund the eventual award in full, were followed by denials that any decision had been taken without knowledge of what the cost would be. In due course a better than parsimonious pay award was recommended and was to be funded in full, but until the last the principle was preserved that review bodies and pay negotiators must not assume that extra money will be found for higher pay without limit. (This exercise was complicated by a change in the grading arrangements for nurses, and the adequacy of the funding was later called into question.)

This snapshot of the situation at a particular date will of course be overtaken by events before it appears in print, but it will remain valid as an illustration of the problems of cash planning. The next illustration is the defence budget which, running at over £19 billion in 1988–89, is the largest programme of 'goods and services' (as distinct from transfer payments such as social security benefits) directly administered by a government Department. This programme has had its ups and downs in recent years. The Conservative government inherited from its Labour predecessor an undertaking given in NATO to increase defence spending by 3 per cent a year in real terms for a period of years: by the end of that period defence expenditure rose to a peak, in real terms, in 1984–85. From one point of view this did not come amiss to a government which attached a high priority to both internal and external security but, as we have seen, it was one of the factors which prevented the government achieving its original objectives for public expenditure as a whole. That has now been corrected; not only has the increase come to an end, but the defence budget for 1988–89 is about £1 billion in real terms below the peak. It is now planned to run level in real terms, though in White Paper newspeak 'provision for defence is being increased.'

There has been some speculation whether this retrenchment

would require another of the defence reviews in which, over the years, the scope of defence commitments has from time to time been reappraised. However, defence spending still remained higher than when this cycle of events began; the services have had the benefit of the improvements made during the period of expansion; and the adjustments which have been necessary so far fall short of anything as drastic as a defence review. But there is a continuing squeeze from the fact that increased provision in 'cost terms', i.e. in terms of the general rate of inflation, amounts to under-provision for actual increases in the pay of the armed forces as well as civilian staff who make up part of the manpower of the support services. The latter are subject to a further squeeze through the operation of running costs, which will be discussed later. From a defence point of view, it is one thing to squeeze headquarters manpower and overheads, but another thing to squeeze the front line capability. The defence scene thus shows some similarity with the situation in the National Health Service, though the problem of differential inflation in the cost of defence equipment is said to have been overcome by changes in the methods of procurement. It is therefore to be inferred that, when we read reports of the large 'additional bids' confronting the Treasury in the annual Survey exercise, they will include a bid from the Ministry of Defence to redress what it sees as under-provision for manpower costs.

Public expenditure on education and science, a little under £19 billion in 1988–89, and planned to run at about the same level in real or cost terms, is not far short of defence spending. But the Department of Education and Science itself is not a big spender by comparison with the Ministry of Defence, since it is local authorities who spend most of the money going to education. It is a curiosity of the system that most of the central government contribution to local authority current expenditure (in which education is the largest item) is provided, not by the DES, but by the Department of the Environment (which is the Department in the lead on local government affairs), and has taken the form of rate support grant towards total 'relevant expenditure' on the whole range of local services. Moreover, though this total is built up from returns of past expenditure and bids for future expenditure on particular services, rate support grant (unlike certain specific grants) is not earmarked for or allocated to individual services in individual local authorities, but has been distributed according to a complex formula related to needs and resources. The character of the grant and the formula for its distribution are to be changed; for the time being I describe the arrangements as they have operated so far.

In a number of ways these arrangements break the rules for the public expenditure Survey as a whole. The consultations with the local authority associations have their own timetable and take place in the summer. The 'baseline' figures in the Autumn Statement and White Paper appear to be of little relevance, if any. The effective starting point appears to be the most recent available figures of actual past expenditure; the end result is the settlement of a total figure of current expenditure in the following year, which will be taken into account in the determination of total rate support grant.

The various central government Departments will then negotiate between themselves an apportionment of the total current expenditure figure to the services for which they are responsible, but it is for practical purposes no more than an illustrative paper allocation. Each local authority determines its own budget in total and its allocation to individual services. This government has adopted a more interventionist approach to local government than any of its predecessors, in particular by rate-capping authorities deemed to be over-spending through raising excessive local rates; but it has not gone so far as to attempt to control local authority spending, service by service, in detail. There is a more direct control of local government capital expenditure through a system of allocations and borrowing approvals for the various capital programmes of each authority, but each one can, in effect, treat the whole of these borrowing approvals as a pool to be drawn upon to meet its requirements at the time; moreover it has a good deal of room for manoeuvre, though not total freedom, in the use of capital receipts from the sale of council houses and other property.

The complexities of local government finance bring to mind the story told of Disraeli, who is supposed to have said: 'Only

three people ever understood the Schleswig-Holstein question –
Bismarck, God Almighty and myself. Now Bismarck is dead and
I have forgotten.' A similar story is told of a particularly obscure
poem of Robert Browning's. And yet, as though by some hidden
hand, the money appears to find its way, in a sense, to the
planned uses, and the system appears to be capable, by and large,
of delivering the intentions of the DES.

In total, however, the current expenditure of local authorities
over a series of years has exceeded by several percentage points
the projected figures in the Autumn Statement and White Paper,
which Departments cannot enforce, though they can influence
the level of spending, mainly through the rate support grant and
the consultations associated with it. From time to time the
Treasury has recognised this reality and has topped up the
planning figures out of the public expenditure reserve, to bring
them into line with actual expenditure, though the rate support
grant has not necessarily been increased correspondingly. To this
extent the term 'planning total' is a misnomer, and the Treasury's
ideas for putting this right are set out in the next chapter. At the
same time, it is arguable that this deficiency in the existing
arrangements, if viewed as a control system, has provided a
safety valve through which local authority education has been
spared something of the squeeze undergone by those bodies
which are directly financed by the DES.

The principal such bodies are the Research Councils, which
account for most of the Science Budget, as it is called, and the
universities, to whom in future the DES money will be
channelled through a new Universities Funding Council. The
effects on the Research Councils of cash planning as currently
operated are illustrated by the following advice on the allocation
of the Science Budget given by the Advisory Board for the
Research Councils in December 1987:

> Relative to the Government's forecasts of inflation in the
> economy as a whole – the GDP deflator – the revised
> expenditure plans for the Science Budget imply ... a slight
> decline: of about 0.2% in each of 1988–89 and 1989–90, with no
> change in 1990–91. However, cost increases affecting the Science
> Budget have for some years exceeded the GDP deflator .... .

Without any further allowance for further cost increases above average inflation, the amount of research which the Science Budget buys will thus be between 2% and 3% lower in 1990–91 than was planned for this year.

It is the universities, however, who appear to have come off worst. In its advice on 'A Strategy for Higher Education Into the 1990s' the University Grants Committee, now to be replaced by the Universities Funding Council, made a plea for

level funding in volume terms – that is, the funding that would be needed to finance the present level of staffing, purchase of books, periodicals, consumables, and so on …. Since pay is the dominant component of university expenditure, accounting for about two-thirds of the total, each fall of 1 per cent in the real income of the university system would mean a fall of at least 1 per cent in the number of staff employed.

In the event, over a period of years, the universities have experienced a volume squeeze on top of outright cuts. The latter are not an automatic consequence of the cash planning system but reflect the original strategy of seeking to reduce public expenditure, the low priority attached by the government to some areas of academic work, and its view that the universities should make themselves less dependent on government money.

This quick look at programmes which account for about two thirds of public expenditure shows that, while circumstances vary from one programme to another, the problem of cost increases above the general level of inflation is common to many of them (with the major exception of social security benefits which keep pace, but no more, with the general price level) and that under-provision for these increases is inherent in the baseline figures used for planning public expenditure under the current rules of the game. This entails a general volume squeeze, on manpower in particular, unless some adjustment is made to the baseline figures, either in the annual re-negotiation of programmes or by an allocation from the public expenditure reserve at some midway point during the year.

If pay rises faster than the general rate of inflation in the private sector, one of the principal factors which make that possible is rising productivity. In the public services also it is logical to do whatever reasonably can be done to offset higher unit manpower costs by higher productivity and economy in the use of manpower. The scope for this will, however, vary from case to case, and there are likely to be cases where an over-prolonged squeeze will make it difficult to preserve standards and will put at risk the continued existence of centres of excellence.

In practice, cash planning as now operated appears to be something of a compromise with volume programming; this is probably inevitable, as the problem of volumes will not disappear. Concessions are made where political realities or negotiating skills or the logic of the government's own priorities can extract something more than the target rate for general inflation. The public expenditure reserve has been increased so as to cope not only with unforeseen contingencies but with foreseeable requirements of this kind. The effects of the system as now operated are uneven but, as compared with the old system of volume planning, control of expenditure and resistance to inflation have without doubt been improved by putting the onus on spending ministers to make out the case for extra money to finance higher costs. As compared with the first uncompromising phase of cash planning, the present compromise represents a shift from dogmatism to pragmatism; but on balance the cash planning system represents a more stringent *regime* than might be suggested by the bare figures of overall increases in public expenditure 'in real terms', adjusted for general but not for differential inflation.

7

The Poll Tax and the Planning Total

Changes in the system for financing local authorities are to take place from 1 April 1989 in Scotland and a year later in England and Wales. What has been said in the previous chapter about the existing system, with particular reference to the education programme, will have to be revised. This chapter summarises the changes and their effects on the Treasury's framing and presentation of public expenditure plans.

At present, meaning mid-1988, local authorities raise part of their current finance by means of the rates, which are a property tax on people's homes (domestic rates) and on commercial and other non-domestic property (business rates).

From 1990 (1989 in Scotland) there will be no more domestic rates. Instead, local authorities will collect a community charge, popularly and more accurately known as a poll tax, i.e. a tax per head. This will be payable by all adults, with certain exceptions, at a flat rate in each area. As a result of this change, the charge will be paid at the same rate by every adult in each household in a local authority area, instead of by the householder alone on the basis of the rateable value of the property. Students will be required to pay only a fifth of the charge, and those on low incomes will be eligible for assistance through the community charge benefit scheme.

The central government's contribution to the generality of current spending on local services will be known as Revenue Support Grant (RSG), retaining the same initials as the old Rate Support Grant. It is stated that the formula for distributing RSG will be greatly simplified because 'RSG will in future need to equalise only assessed differences in needs, e.g. the age structure of the population.' It will not have to allow for variations in rateable values across the country. Specific central government grants, such as the police grant, will continue.

Business rates will continue, but in England and Wales the proceeds will be paid into a pool operated by central government, and will be paid out to all local authorities on a per capita basis; there is to be a uniform poundage (i.e. a uniform rate of payment by businesses in relation to the value of their property) which will be indexed in line with inflation. The arrangements in Scotland will be a little different.

Thus, each local authority's funds for current spending from central or local government taxation will consist of the proceeds of the community charge, plus its share of business rates, plus Revenue Support Grant, plus specific grants. It is stated that 'The effect of these arrangements will be to ensure that each pound per adult more or less that a local authority spends will add to or reduce community charge bills by one pound.' This will be in line with a principal objective of the new system, that is, to make local voters feel the consequences of the spending decisions of the councillors whom they elect, and thus to discourage excessive spending. Another objective has been to rescue businesses from the sometimes swingeing rate increases imposed by local authorities which, as businesses, they play no part in electing. The objections to the new arrangements rest largely on grounds of equity, since the community charge will be a highly regressive tax, bearing no relation to means and ability to pay, except through the benefit system at the bottom end of the income range. Affluent householders stand to benefit; less affluent families stand to pay more. It is also argued that there will be a disincentive for people to register for the charge, if they are prepared to disenfranchise themselves in order to avoid being on the list of local residents.

As regards the capital expenditure of local authorities, this is to be regulated by a new system of credit approvals. Each authority's credit approvals will be determined in the following way. Departments responsible for each of the main service blocks will issue annual 'capital guidelines' (analogous to capital allocations under the old system) to the local authorities concerned. These 'capital guidelines' for each service for which the authority is responsible will be added up. An allowance (or one might say disallowance) for the authority's ability to use capital receipts will be deducted. Credit approvals will be issued for the sum of the capital guidelines *less* the allowance for capital receipts.

The Treasury has used these changes as the occasion for redefining the public expenditure planning total so as to exclude that part of local authority current expenditure which is financed by local taxation and which central government cannot effectively determine – a change which it has aimed to make for some time. The inclusion of this expenditure and its attribution on paper to particular programmes – education, roads, etc. – used to produce some nonsenses in the old days, when spending ministers, required to contribute to public expenditure cuts, would blithely offer cuts in local authority current expenditure on 'their' programmes, secure in the knowledge that these would be only paper cuts in paper programmes. In more recent years it has been a matter of chagrin to the Treasury that the planning total could appear to be exceeded, and a charge had to be scored against the public expenditure reserve, because of the behaviour of this joker in the pack.

The proposed redefinition is explained in a White Paper issued in July 1988 with the title *A New Public Expenditure Planning Total*. The planning total does not correspond to the expenditure side of the Budget, nor is it a recognised statistical aggregate in general use. (The figures of General Government Expenditure (GGE) come closer to that, and are used for tracing the progress of public expenditure in relation to GDP; these statistics will be unaffected by the redefinition of the planning total.) The planning total is an aggregate specially constructed to suit the purposes of the public expenditure Survey system, and includes some items which at first sight are rather disparate in other respects.

'The main criterion,' says the White Paper, 'for including a class of expenditure within the new planning total is whether central government can be said to have responsibility for determining the level of that expenditure.' Strictly speaking, some of the elements in the planning total are not expenditure as such, but financing items, mainly borrowing, which do duty for the expenditure thus financed.

Central government's own expenditure, that is, money spent directly by government Departments and the National Health Service, will make up the bulk of the planning total, as it does now. On the local government front, central government grants to local authorities (RSG plus specific grants plus capital grants plus grants to cover community charge benefit) and also local authority credit approvals and non-domestic rate payments from the national pool – in other words, all the elements in local government finance which will be regulated by central government, instead of, as now, the whole expenditure programmes of the local authorities – will come within the new planning total. Current expenditure which the local authorities finance themselves, from the proceeds of the community charge or other receipts such as trading surpluses, will be outside the planning total (though still within the statistics of General Government Expenditure).

The planning total on the new basis is to feature for the first time in the 1989 public expenditure survey, the results of which will be announced in the 1989 Autumn Statement. This will set out plans for the various grants to local authorities, and for the new-style credit approvals, for three years ahead, instead of one as at present. The Revenue Support Grant will be shown as a Department of the Environment programme (or a Scottish or Welsh Office programme) since it is the DOE which pays out RSG in England, even though it goes to support a range of services with which other Departments are concerned. Specific grants will be shown as part of the programmes of those Departments. These will be the Central government's planning figures. But projections will be made of total local government expenditure, including that part which they finance themselves, and will form part of projected General Government Expenditure.

These arrangements recognise that central government will not have control over that part of the spending of the local authorities which is financed out of community charge at a level which the local electorate are prepared to bear, or against which they are not energetic enough to vote. Advocates of a degree of local self-government will consider that that is as it should be. Nevertheless the White Paper contains the following minatory statement: 'But if the Government felt that this expenditure was growing too rapidly ... the Government would need to consider whether to take action to moderate the growth of expenditure within the planning total, whether its own spending or grants to local authorities.' This can be taken as a warning that the new planning total involves only changes in technique, not in the strategy of reducing General Government Expenditure – whether spent by central or local government – as a percentage of GDP.

In addition to central and local government, the planning total covers the public corporations, including the nationalised industries. For these, the planning total scores, not their expenditure – which, since they are trading organisations, it would not be sensible to try to control – but their external finance, 'whether this is raised from Government by grant or loan, or through market or overseas borrowing.' While some of the nationalised industries have required large injections of external finance in the form of government subsidies, others have made surpluses sufficient to repay debt or accumulate funds, and have thus had negative requirements of external finance, which have scored as reductions in the planning total; the electricity supply industry in England and Wales, for instance, currently scores a minus figure of over £1 billion. For a monopoly public utility, such surpluses are essentially a function of the prices they charge, which in turn derive from the required rate of return on their assets. (Another reason why the electricity industry has had a negative requirement for external finance has been its relatively low investment during a period of over-capacity from which it is only now emerging.)

To these items we should add the public expenditure reserve and deduct privatisation proceeds, which are treated as negative expenditure. Central government debt interest is outside the planning total since, as such, it is not an item which can be determined by Cabinet, but is the product of the whole of fiscal and monetary policy; between them these determine the amount of government borrowing and the rates of interest on it. (Debt interest paid by local authorities has, however, an indirect effect on the new planning total, since it forms part of the current expenditure which attracts RSG.) The White Paper on the planning total has a table with illustrative figures recast to show how the new planning total will be made up. I have further rearranged this material in table 1 so as to show the structure of the new planning total in simplified form.

The new planning total will bring together for decision by Cabinet all the expenditure programmes within their powers of direct control together with various programmes indirectly controlled by other (non-expenditure) financial limits. It is not a homogeneous statistical aggregate, and might perhaps be better designated as the public *sector* (rather than public expenditure) planning total, but it is a means of requiring all these items to run in the same competition for funds within the available total – something which has to be done by one means or another in the allocation of resources and determination of priorities in the non-market sector.

It might be argued that the rules of the competition should be altered so as to cover only those services for which the government provides the money, thus excluding capital expenditure which the local authorities finance by market borrowing or from capital receipts. But clearly no government in present circumstances would be prepared to give local authorities a totally free hand on capital expenditure; since the government retains control, there is a case for bringing this particular requirement within the same planning framework as other capital requirements in the non-market sector.

The case for including the external finance of the public corporations which are in the market sector seems to me more dubious. The implication is that, in the last analysis, a choice might be made between, say, cutting the defence budget and raising electricity prices so as to generate a larger negative figure of external finance; at times in the past this has been a not unrealistic hypothesis. However, if the privatisation programme

Table 1   The planning total: illustrative figures

	(£ billion) 1988–89 (plans)
Items included in the planning total	
Central government:	
central government's own expenditure	114.2
grants to local authorities	22.8
Other local authority items:	
national non-domestic rate payments	10.0
local authority credit approvals	3.9
Public corporations' external finance	1.4
Reserve	2.5
	154.8
Less privatisation proceeds	5.0
New planning total	149.9*
Items not included in the planning total	
local authority self-financed expenditure	10.4
central government debt interest	17.7
accounting adjustments	4.8
	32.9
General government expenditure	183.0*

Note: The total for local authorities is £47.1 billion, of
which £36.8 billion is included in the planning
total.

*The totals are affected by rounding of the individual
items.

runs its full course, all the more profitable nationalised industries
will have disappeared from the planning total; the main items
left in will be the subsidies for coal, the railways and London
Regional Transport, all of which properly belong in any
definition of public expenditure. Time should therefore resolve
this issue, along with much else.

8

The Treasury and Parliament

In July 1981 the Select Committee on Procedure (Supply) reported that the whole of the financial procedures of the House of Commons were 'antiquated and defective and need a thorough overhaul'. It made recommendations which it described as 'a real opportunity for the House to begin to reassert its historic function of scrutinising and controlling public expenditure'.

But this phraseology runs together two very different things. The distinction was recognised in a later report by the Select Committee on Procedure (Finance): 'While we reject the concept of a binding *control* by the House over the totality of public expenditure, we believe that there should be more scope for effective *scrutiny* ....'

The same committee commented that 'Many of the House's procedures and practices derive from a period when the Crown obtained most of its revenue from sources not dependent on annual Parliamentary consent. Grants from Parliament were essentially supplementary and were provided, if at all, only following a request from the Crown.' Now that the days are long past when the monarch could pay for the armed forces largely out of the revenue from the Crown estates, and public expenditure is equivalent to around 40 per cent of a vastly expanded national income, the question is in what sense can Parliament reasonably be expected to control either the expenditure side of the Budget or the Budget as a whole.

As things stand, while Parliament controls a great many things, such as capital punishment and the times when we may drink in public houses and when women may have abortions, it has only formal control over part of public expenditure and none at all over the rest. It approves tax changes in the annual Finance Bill, but it has no right of approval of government borrowing. Thus it has formal rights in relation to part of the expenditure side of the Budget and part of its financing side, but it does not exercise these rights at the same time, and so it never votes on the Budget as a whole.

Let us digress for a moment to the position in Cabinet, where there is an even more complete dichotomy between the procedures relating to public expenditure on the one hand and its financing on the other. Cabinet, as we have seen, is deeply involved in settling the expenditure which makes up the 'planning total'. In the nature of things, it would hardly be feasible to determine expenditure programmes without involving the spending ministers who are responsible for them, but it is a feature of the Cabinet system as operated in this field that ministers are involved collectively, instead of confining the process to separate negotiations with individual ministers, as normally happens in France. The present procedures for collective Cabinet involvement in expenditure decisions date back to the introduction in the 1960s of the Survey system, whose architects misguidedly imagined that wider ministerial participation in the process would breed a greater sense of responsibility and encourage greater restraint, whereas the actual result has been to make life more difficult for the Treasury.

The Treasury has never had any illusions that it would be a good thing to involve Cabinet in taxation matters. Although there is usually an occasion for a general discussion of the economic background to the Budget some time before Budget day – an occasion which is, however, not of a decision-making character – Cabinet is given a preview of the tax measures in the Budget only on the morning of the great day itself. Since the expenditure decisions have by then been taken and promulgated, the Budget proposals are about taxation and borrowing. The Red Book presents the figures on both expenditure and receipts, but the former are at this stage old hat unless, exceptionally, the Chancellor uses the Budget speech to announce some late changes in the expenditure allocations. As a result, the term 'Budget' is often associated solely with the announcement of tax changes in the spring. Sometimes a change in interest rates may be announced at Budget time, but not as part of the Budget proper.

All the things which are at the heart of economic management – the Budget balance, interest rates and the exchange rate – are in practice matters for the Chancellor under our system, in consultation with the Governor of the Bank of England on interest rates and the exchange rate, and reporting to the Prime Minister who, over at least the last few administrations, has had the last word. (Roy Jenkins, however, consulted Harold Wilson hardly at all on the Budget.) These derogations from the doctrine of collective Cabinet responsibility go back as far as one can remember and have nothing to do with the alleged recent Presidential style of government. A closer analogy might be drawn with the running of large companies, in which a line is drawn between those matters which go to the Board of Directors as a whole and those which are a matter solely for management. Where precisely the line is drawn varies according to the management style of the company and the personalities in the key positions; in some companies a rather generous view is taken of the matters which are the prerogative of management and a rather restrictive view of the role of the Board. So long as management deliver satisfactory results in terms of profits and dividends, they are in a strong position and unlikely to be challenged.

Budgetary procedures can vary from country to country. In some countries at least the Budget as a whole goes to Cabinet for approval. This would, for instance, tend to happen in European countries with coalition governments, in which policy has to be cleared with all the coalition partners.

Let us return now to the role of Parliament, which in this context means the House of Commons, since the House of Lords formally ceased to have any say in national money matters in 1911, and is judged to have ceased to do so *de facto* before then. The House of Commons is not involved at all in the public expenditure Survey until the results are presented to it, initially in the Autumn Statement (and later in more detail about individual programmes) when the House is invited to take note with approval, or some such phrase. Neither the Autumn Statement nor the follow-up documents are the vehicle for formal authorisation of the expenditure by Parliament; the required authorisation is given by means of a Supply procedure which has its roots in history.

Estimates of the money required for each service are presented to Parliament by the Financial Secretary to the Treasury. Under the current revised procedures, a number of Estimates are selected for debate on the recommendation of the Departmentally related Select Committees (which will be discussed in more detail a little later on) and on the basis of reports from them. The selection is made by a Liaison Committee consisting of the chairmen of the Select Committees. Three days in each Parliamentary session are set aside to debate the selected Estimates, which are then approved by voting on Supply resolutions, or Estimates resolutions as they are now often called. By convention the House can in principle reduce an Estimate – which in practice it does not succeed in doing – but it cannot increase one, since under our conventions only the executive can initiate expenditure. The rest of the Estimates, i.e. those not selected for debate, are agreed to by a single blanket resolution.

The three days allocated for these selective debates replace fifteen Supply days which used to be available for dealing with Estimates as a whole, but which were felt to be ineffective, and which could be used for debating any subject of the opposition's choice. The belief is that more will be achieved through the new-style debates, which are better focused and better prepared through the Select Committee reports. The change can be seen as a move away from going through the motions of control towards more effective scrutiny.

It is perhaps a moot point, not put to the test, whether Supply (or Estimates) Resolutions by themselves are sufficient authority for the issue of the money involved. In practice, authority to issue money is secured by passing a Consolidated Fund Act. Supplementary Estimates and further Consolidated Fund Acts can be approved as required in the course of the year. Final legislative authority for the specific amounts devoted to specific services is given by means of an Appropriation Act.

The generality of the public services are covered by these Supply procedures, which retain their importance as the only means of authorising the spending of taxpayers' money on these services, but there is also a substantial part of public money which goes through other channels. Social security benefits come only in part out of Estimates and the Consolidated Fund, into which all tax revenue is paid; the rest of the money for social security comes out of the National Insurance Fund, into which national insurance contributions by employers and employees are paid. There are certain other payments which are issued directly out of the Consolidated Fund, without the benefit of Estimates, because they are regarded as absolute obligations which cannot be subjected to the hazards of the Supply procedures.

The largest of these direct issues are the service of the national debt (that is, interest paid on all accumulated outstanding government borrowings) and our contributions to the European Community. Parliament has in the past approved the legislation setting up these procedures, but the legislation left it with no say in the payments year by year. Similarly, Parliament has enacted the arrangements for government borrowing and lending through the National Loans Fund, and it has set overall limits on the amounts lent for certain purposes, but it has no say in the amounts borrowed and lent each year. It is in the annual Survey that all the categories of payments, whether Supply or non-Supply expenditure, come together.

Inside Whitehall, the role of Estimates has been changed by the development of the Survey system. Before this system was introduced, it was through the Estimates that Departments made their bids and through the processing of Estimates by the Treasury that the annual expenditure battle was fought out. In 1958 Peter Thorneycroft, a reluctant martyr, resigned as Chancellor of the Exchequer after Cabinet rejected his attempt, not supported by the Prime Minister, Harold Macmillan, to cut Estimates by £50 million. Since the Survey system has become the decision-making exercise, Estimates have become the mechanism for the translation of these decisions into control figures, so far as the money involved takes the form of Supply expenditure; though still a painstaking process, this is a matter of detail rather than of policy. A latter-day Thorneycroft would make his stand in the course of the Survey exercise, not at the Estimates stage.

A need therefore became felt for means by which the Commons could monitor public expenditure going beyond the Supply procedures. A certain malaise about the role of the House of Commons was not confined to the financial front. There has been, for some years now, some dissatisfaction among backbenchers, including the government's backbench supporters in the Commons, at their largely passive role. The occasional free vote on capital punishment or on a Private Member's Bill about abortion is a relatively rare occasion. More commonly, backbenchers go through the division lobby to vote for (or, in the case of the Opposition, against) measures decided upon by the government.

The present Select committee system has been developed largely with a view to giving backbenchers a somewhat less frustrating role. In 1979 the new government gave effect to a recommendation which had been put forward in the previous Parliament, but not decided upon by the outgoing government, to replace the previous 'specialist' Select Committees, dealing with subjects such as Science and Technology or Nationalised Industries, with a number of Select Committees, each monitoring the affairs of one or more particular Departments. Thus the former Expenditure Committee, which itself had replaced the old and less comprehensive Estimates Committee, but which had continued to chafe at the limitations of its remit, was replaced by a Treasury and Civil Service Committee, with an unrestricted remit to inquire into and report on policies on the Treasury front.

The prevailing mood when the new Select Committees were set up was hopeful; there was a belief that they would play a more effective and influential role. Up to a point, the psychology of the change, as well as the new focus on the affairs of particular Departments, has given the Select Committees a higher profile, and places on them are much sought after. Each committee is serviced by a Clerk to the Committee, who is a member of the permanent staff of the House of Commons, and assisted by academics, consultants and so on serving as specialist advisers. Ministers and officials are quizzed in great detail; the reports produced can be a mine of information and are often newsworthy. The attendance and input of committee members is variable, but a good committee chairman, with the right support from the Clerk to the Committee and the advisers, can go a long way to make up for that.

Reports from the Treasury and Civil Service Committee provide a foundation for debates on public expenditure as a whole on the floor of the House of Commons. Other Departmentally related committees have become the instrument for scrutinising and reporting on individual expenditure programmes. The House is now, to put it at its lowest, better equipped to monitor all the expenditure covered by the annual Survey – not merely Supply expenditure – and to require the government to account for its policies.

Inevitably, given our Parliamentary system, limitations on the role and performance of the Select Committees remain. Beyond a certain point, they cannot rise above the party system. The fact that all parties are represented on the committees is both a strength and a limitation. If a unanimous report can be secured, it will have a greater claim to consideration and carry more weight with the public. But there is usually a point beyond which government supporters on a committee will not go in outright criticism of government policy in a committee report. Political squabbles about representation on the committees have delayed their reconstitution after the last two general elections, and this has not enhanced the esteem in which they are held by the informed public.

But the essential limitation is that the new Select Committees have no rights of approval of government measures, and no direct role in the decision-making process, any more than the old committees had. In a discussion about the value of Select Committees, a well-known journalist asked, 'What decision has ever been changed by a Select Committee report?', to which a well-known minister replied 'What decision has ever been

changed by one of your leading articles?' The implication was
that the Select Committees help to form the climate of opinion in
which decisions are taken. No minister would, I think,
gratuitously expose himself to a hostile grilling or a critical
report by a Select Committee, and it is arguable that this gives
them a more direct influence than the press on government
attitudes, short of changing their decisions. A revolt among the
government's supporters, if they are prepared to follow it
through in the division lobby, is more capable of having that
effect, on rare occasions.

The creation of the Treasury and Civil Service Committee did
not disarm criticism of the fragmented nature of Parliament's
role in the Budget process as a whole. As we have seen, this
fragmentation is twofold – expenditure and its financing are not
taken together; and the processes of annual authorisation do not
apply to the whole of expenditure or the whole of its financing.
But how far are these really matters for concern?

Proposals for Budgetary reform were put forward in 1980 by a
committee under the chairmanship of the late William
Armstrong, formerly a Permanent Secretary to the Treasury and
Head of the Home Civil Service, and at the time a life peer with
the title Lord Armstrong of Sanderstead. The committee was
convened by the Institute of Fiscal Studies and was not an
exclusively Parliamentary committee, but included outsiders
also. It recommended that a 'Green' or provisional Budget
should be presented in November or December, which could be
scrutinised by an appropriate committee and debated in the
House, followed by a 'White' or actual Budget at a later date.
Both the provisional and the actual Budget would be an
integrated document, containing revenue and expenditure
proposals together. These recommendations were taken up and
supported by the Treasury and Civil Service Committee, and by
the Select Committee on Procedure (Finance).

The objective of these proposals was to expose both sides of
the Budget to simultaneous scrutiny at a stage when it was still
possible to vary the tax and expenditure proposals. Even if one
supported the objective, the idea of traversing the whole ground
twice over – at the 'Green Budget' stage and then at the 'White

Budget' stage – took no account of the vast amount of work, thought and negotiating effort which is required to do these things even once, and would have been an extremly laborious business. But in any case the Treasury was never a party to that objective.

In the British context, the proposed changes amounted not to reform but to revolution, since they would have given the Commons or its Select Committees powers to vet the Budget in advance which are at present denied even to Cabinet. If they were adopted, it would hardly be possible to maintain indefinitely the present exclusive rights of the Prime Minister and the Chancellor in budgetary matters *vis-à-vis* the rest of Cabinet. The proposed reforms would have radically tipped the balance both between Parliament and the executive and between the top management and the rest of the executive.

Envious glances are frequently cast, by those who do not care for this state of affairs, in the direction of the United States where management, in the person of the President, has to share power with Congress, which has real authority and a large bureaucracy of its own to help in the exercise of its authority. However, in recent years that system has permitted a massive and intractable budget deficit. 'At least,' I have heard a United States official say, after commenting on the divorce between the procedures on the expenditure side and on the revenue side in the British system, 'At least you can make a Budget.'

It was in response to the recommendations for Armstrong-type reform that the Treasury put forward the proposal for the Autumn Statement, which has since then become an increasingly important part of the budgetary cycle. In its original form, the 1982 Autumn Statement went a long way, though not the whole way, towards giving the House a preview of the Budget which it could expect in the following spring. The detailed appraisal of the economic prospects for the year ahead provides the same kind of material as that on which the Treasury itself must form its judgement on the state of the economy as background to the Budget; in this respect the character of the Autumn Statement remains unchanged. In another respect it now goes further than in 1982, when outline plans for public expenditure were given for only one year ahead, whereas since 1985 planned programmes have been shown for the whole Survey period; we can expect this part of the document to be developed further in subsequent years. But when we come to the receipts side of the Budget, glasnost has gone into reverse.

That is to say, the 1982 Autumn Statement gave projections not only of spending but also of revenue and borrowing in the following year, leading up to a projected 'fiscal adjustment', which was a forecast of the tax reductions or expenditure increases which the Chancellor might be able to afford when Budget time came around. It also contained a ready reckoner of the amounts involved in illustrative tax changes. The Chancellor of the Exchequer, at that time Sir Geoffrey Howe, said that in his view the Autumn Statement provided 'a pretty good Do-it-Yourself Budget kit'. However, under Nigel Lawson, the projections of receipts and of the fiscal adjustment have disappeared from the Autumn Statement, no doubt on the grounds that too much can change between the autumn and the spring to make it sensible for the Chancellor to try to anticipate his Budget in this particular way.

The upshot of this experiment with reform has therefore been to bring forward into the autumn the occasion when the spotlight is turned on the public expenditure plans and to separate expenditure even further from the taxation side of the Budget. Although both sides of the equation are presented in the Red Book at Budget time, the expenditure plans are by then, in the main, a *fait accompli*.

This does not mean that the two sides of the equation are never brought together before the preparation of the Red Book. The Treasury must bring them together, in one way or another, in its work on the medium-term strategy and in shorter-term projections. But Parliament does not get these figures. The experiment in providing a preview of the Budget balance in the Autumn Statement did not last very long, as we have seen. How, it is asked, can the House make an informed judgement on the government's expenditure plans in isolation from its plans for taxation and borrowing? It is also arguable that, under the present system, the expenditure decisions can be taken without regard to their consequences for taxation and borrowing, that the Budget will therefore be expenditure-led, and that this did in fact happen in the 1970s and led to the era of high taxation and high public borrowing.

The Treasury's answer would have to be, I think, that – whatever may have gone wrong in the past – under the present management the public expenditure exercise does not take place nor are the results presented in a void, but in the context of the medium term financial strategy and the declared objectives of cutting taxation, restraining public borrowing, and reducing public expenditure as a proportion of GDP. An answer on these lines would be unlikely to persuade everybody; but so long as the Chancellor can go on delivering results which are satisfactory to at least the government's supporters, he is unlikely to come under effective pressure for further moves in the direction of the Armstrong proposals. We can, however, expect to see continuing improvements in presentation; these in turn should further facilitate the processes of scrutiny.

In strategic planning, nothwithstanding all its uncertainties and limitations, clearly both sides of the equation have to be looked at together. When it comes to specific expenditure decisions for the year ahead, there are good management reasons, in the British context, for taking these in advance of specific taxation decisions. The former involve spending Departments, local authorities and other public bodies, all of which need to know, well in advance of the financial year, the basis on which they can frame their own budgets for the year. Changes in social security benefits and contributions also require several months notice – for instance, in order to print and distribute new pension books.

The main taxes, on the other hand, are directly under the Chancellor's control. (Exceptions are Vehicle Excise Duty, for which the Department of Transport is responsible, and local authority taxation, previously in the form of rates on property, which it is planned to replace by a poll tax described as a Community Charge.) The Chancellor can decide on changes in direct taxes and (subject to any constraints arising from our membership of the European Community) indirect taxes at a date much closer to Budget day, perhaps only a few days before. When it comes to the announcement of these changes, Chancellors have been known to continue drafting changes in the Budget speech up to the very morning of Budget day, amid mounting anxiety in their Private Office and Press Office. From the Chancellor's point of view, there are advantages in making his Budget judgement as close to the event as possible, on the basis of the latest appraisal of the economy and the most up-to-date forecasts of receipts and outgoings. It is likely that, if tax changes had to be decided upon and announced in the autumn, they would be different from the changes made in the spring.

In spite of these practical considerations, there is nevertheless room for unease about the absence of effective procedures for even debating expenditure and taxation together. It seems to me less bothersome that the Supply procedures do not cover the whole of public expenditure. The Survey results, which do cover all expenditure, Supply and non-Supply, are there for scrutiny and debate. This will not satisfy any who still hanker for something more in the way of control. The 1983 report of the Select Committee on Procedure (Finance) included the following:

At present the only overall 'control' is a Vote in the House each year to approve or disapprove the plans set out in the Public Expenditure White Paper. In no real sense can this be described as a control. A Government which was defeated on this vote would be under no legal requirement to alter its spending plans or to resign, as was shown when a defeat occurred in March 1976. This is in marked contrast to the consequences if the Government had lost a Supply vote; it would not get the money for which it had asked, and it might have to resign.

However, on that occasion in 1976, when Labour rebels, disgruntled with cuts in expenditure programmes, joined with the Opposition to vote against Denis Healey's White Paper – provoking his classic remark that they were out of their tiny Chinese minds – the government responded by tabling a vote of confidence the next day. This time the rebels joined in the vote of confidence, rather than see the Labour government fall, as it would have been obliged to do, under the rules of the game, in the event of losing a vote of confidence.

Thus the house has as much or as little control over the government's expenditure plans as a whole as it has over any other major government measure; if it is prepared to carry its objections *à outrance*, and a sufficient number of the government's own supporters are prepared to vote against it, it can bring the government down.

This is a most unlikely scenario. Even the Select Committee on the Treasury and Civil Service, if it ever had any real expectations of powers of control, appears to have settled for rights of scrutiny. As things stand, this committee can scrutinise and report on expenditure plans as a whole, as a basis for debate by the House of Commons, while other Select Committees can scrutinise and report on Departmental programmes, as a basis for debate in connection with the approval of Estimates. In response to suggestions from the Treasury and Civil Service Committee, the Treasury has now tabled proposals which should enhance the scrutiny of Departmental expenditure plans.

Under these proposals, which are likely to be largely in effect by the time this book is published, the present series of three documents (Autumn Statement, Public Expenditure White Paper and Estimates) would be rationalised into two. The Autumn Statement would become the sole presentation of the government's overall expenditure plans and policies; it would be expanded to include as much as possible of the key material from chapter 1 of the White Paper (which is part of Volume I of that document). Volume II of the White Paper would be split into separate Departmental volumes containing each Department's plans; these would be published in March, on or before Budget day, in conjunction with the formal Supply Estimates. The remaining material in Volume I might be made available in a number of ways, for example as a statistical supplement to the previously published Autumn Statement.

How, it may be asked, will it make for improved scrutiny if Volume II of the White Paper is replaced by a number of Departmental volumes, except that the latter will be handier for the Departmental Select Committees, and for the Treasury itself, since the existing Part II is now so full of information that it is bursting at the seams? One improvement will arise from the fact that this splitting up of the White Paper information will be married with other moves to align this information more closely with the Estimates figures, so that it will be easier to read across from each new Departmental volume to the corresponding volume of Estimates. The two sets of figures will not, however, be identical in all cases, because a good many programmes include both Supply expenditure and non-Supply expenditure which is not in Estimates. Beyond this, the hope is that the change will encourage the supply of even more data and analysis, enabling the Select Committees to make an assessment of value for money, not after the event like the Public Accounts Committee and the National Audit Office, but at the planning stage when, unlike those other bodies, the Committees will be under no restraints on questioning policy objectives.

9

The Committee on Public Accounts and the National Audit Office

The audit function is of even greater importance in the public services than it is in the company sector and it now goes far wider. An effective system of value for money audit is one of the instruments which have to be used in the non-market sector in lieu of the profit and loss criterion.

The accounts of government Departments, unlike company accounts, are not audited by commercial firms of auditors but by a body set up for this specific purpose. There have been commissions of one kind or another to look into government accounts, either on an *ad hoc* or a continuing basis, over many centuries. The present arrangements stem from the creation, by statute, of the office of Comptroller and Auditor General in 1866, at first as head of the Exchequer and Audit Department and later, since 1984, of the National Audit Office. The 'Comptroller' part of this august title means that, in one of his capacities, he authorises the issue of public funds to government Departments and other public bodies, but this is only a minor part of the duties of the office.

Although the Exchequer and Audit Department came under the aegis of the Committee of Public Accounts – more commonly known as the Public Accounts Committee or PAC – as does the National Audit Office today, it was a civil service body and the number and pay of its staff were controlled by the central Departments in the same way as the rest of the civil service. The E&AD was independent in its enquiries and findings, like its successor body, and in choosing its programme of work, though in my day it used to consult the Treasury about this.

The work of the Exchequer and Audit Department used to be described as 'account based', in that the bedrock of its work was the auditing and certification of Appropriation Accounts, trading accounts, and so on; but increasingly it came to concern itself, not only with such things as waste or over-payment or misuse of public money, but also with value for money in the implementation of government policies – though not with the merits of the policies themselves. After agreement of the factual content of each report with the Department concerned, the Comptroller and Auditor General would put the report to the Public Accounts Committee. In due course the committee would summon the senior official designated as Accounting Officer, usually the Permanent Secretary of the spending Department, to quiz him on the report; finally the PAC would present its own report to the House of Commons.

It has always been a matter of great importance to spending Departments to avoid a black mark from the C&AG and the Public Accounts Committee on any question of regularity or propriety in its stewardship of public money. The Treasury has an official at Under Secretary level called the Treasury Officer of Accounts, who is the link man with the PAC and the NAO, and with the Exchequer and Audit Department before it; he is also the custodian of precedents and the repository of wisdom in these matters, and advises Departments (usually through the Treasury Division which is their usual contact) on any such matters referred to him. A warning from him that the C&AG and the Public Accounts Committee would be likely to criticise the propriety of a particular arrangement would be enough to deter a spending Department from that course. Traditionally, the Treasury regarded the Exchequer and Audit Department and itself as being on the same side; it also felt itself to have a special relationship with the Public Accounts Committee.

The relationship is rather different for a Permanent Secretary who is an Accounting Officer for a Departmental Appropriation Account. An appearance before the Public Accounts Committee can be something of an ordeal for him. By tradition, he goes into retreat for several days beforehand to study the account and the C&AG's report on it and to swot up the briefs prepared for him within the Department. It is quite likely, especially in a large Department, that this will be the first that he has heard of some of the things done in his Department's name. Because of the time-lags involved, someone else may have been Permanent Secretary and Accounting Officer when the events in question took place, but it is the current Accounting Officer who has to answer for them.

The PAC's role in these matters has always given it a more specific function (i.e. the oversight of public accounts) and a more extensive back-up (from the C&AG and his staff) than the Select Committees discussed in the previous chapter; in consequence the PAC has had a higher standing and greater clout. The position of chairman of the PAC, which is occupied by a senior politician from the Opposition benches, is highly regarded. The Committee has been an arbiter of propriety and regularity in the use of public money. A finding by the C&AG and the Public Accounts Committee of outright waste or over-spending could not be ignored.

In 1983, following recommendations by the Public Accounts Committee, and in response to a good deal of backbench pressure – an aspect of the recurring pressure for a more effective role for the House of Commons – the National Audit Act was passed and took effect the following year. This has brought about changes of greater significance than may at first have been imagined, given that there was a large element of continuity of functions and procedures. As part of these changes, the existing Comptroller and Auditor General became an officer of the House of Commons and would in future consult the PAC, not the Treasury, about his programme of work; and he became head of the National Audit Office, which replaced the Exchequer and Audit Department. The staff of the new body, more then 800 in number, were no longer civil servants. The budget of the National Audit Office came under the supervision of a newly established Public Accounts Commission of the House of Commons; it is therefore immune to cuts made in the civil service. The remit of the NAO was extended to cover not only government Departments but a wider range than before of other bodies in receipt of public money; but the nationalised industries, after a good deal of negotiation, were excluded. The House had to back down on this point, or otherwise the government, under other pressures from the heads of the nationalised industries and their sponsor Departments, would have blocked the whole Bill.

Under the 1983 Act, the C&AG was for the first time given the statutory function of carrying out value for money audits or, in the words of the Act, 'examinations into the economy, efficiency and effectiveness with which any department ... has used its resources in discharging its functions'. But this was 'not to be construed as entitling the Comptroller and Auditor General to question the merits of the policy objectives of any department ....'

Value for money audits were not a break with the past, but the statutory recognition of this function was, and so was the change of style adopted by the National Audit Office and its head. An attractive format has been adopted for its reports, which are free from officialese and are introduced by a punchy summary. Each report is published, with a press notice, and presented to the House of Commons in advance of its consideration by the PAC. The new body has aimed at and achieved a much higher profile.

The work of the National Audit Office is still, in a sense, 'account-based', in that it still has the basic task of auditing and certifying Departmental and certain other accounts. But it is doubtful whether its value for money examinations have any close connection with a Department's accounts or emerge naturally from the conventional audit activity; it might be more accurate to say that the familiarity with a Department which the NAO gains from this work puts it in a good position to select and pursue subjects of interest from a value-for-money point of view.

The nearest analogies to these pieces of work in the company sector are to be found in the reports of management consultants rather than of company auditors, though the same firm of accountants may provide both services. But management consultants are more usually engaged to advise on some specific problem rather than to roam at will over a whole organisation.

Their reports are not published and are made to the management of the organisation itself, not to, say, the shareholders nor to any body remotely corresponding to the House of Commons and the PAC. This is just one illustration of the differences between the market and the non-market sectors.

In the commercial world the relationship of a firm of accountants with a company is one of confidentiality and trust. The National Audit Office, on the other hand, as it has moved further away from the account-based approach, has found that its new role and higher profile have brought with them some problems in relationships with Whitehall. These relationships are not analogous to those of a company's professional advisers, because the NAO makes its reports not to Whitehall but to the House of Commons and, in particular, the Public Accounts Committee. The latter has stated its desire to continue the tradition of reports agreed between the C&AG and the spending Department, but it is much harder for them to agree the text of a new-style report with a greater content of appraisal, judgement and opinion. After some initial misunderstanding of what was expected, efforts have been made to work out acceptable forms of words going beyond the purely factual element in a report, but this is time-consuming and difficult, and at the end of the day a Department may still feel that its reservations about the NAO's comments are inadequately reflected.

Moreover, as seen from Whitehall, the NAO has from the first been pushing at the frontiers of its remit and encroaching on policy issues – an encroachment which, from the point of view of the executive, has to be discouraged if the National Audit Office and the Committee on Public Accounts are not to develop into a court of appeal sitting in judgment on government policies. The National Audit Office and the Treasury are still on the same side in that they are both concerned with the proper application of public funds and value for money, but the NAO's reports have sometimes seemed to the Treasury to be arguing for more resources in order to make policies more effective, whereas government policy requires standards of service to be constrained by the available resources.

Whitehall does not respond formally to NAO reports as such,

but to the subsequent PAC report, by means of a Treasury
Minute submitted on behalf of the Treasury and the spending
Department jointly. However, the PAC report takes the NAO
report as its starting point and is drafted by the NAO.
Notwithstanding the Treasury's special relationship with the
PAC, its problems with the new-style reports have been bound to
affect its responses to some PAC reports. It is, for instance,
difficult to recollect any rejection of PAC recommendations in
earlier days on a par with the response by the Treasury, jointly
with the Foreign and Commonwealth Office and the
Department of Trade and Industry, to a 1987 PAC report on the
export promotion services of the latter Departments. The report
recommended 'that there should be a fundamental re-appraisal of
the export promotion services of the FCO and DTI, aimed at
clarifying their strategic objectives; establishing the numbers and
types of staff to do the job effectively, on a demand-led rather
than a resource-led basis.' Whether or not this was a reasonable
point of view, it was bound to strike Whitehall as at odds with
the stipulation that the C&AG is not entitled to question the
policy objectives of any Department; it also appeared to
disregard the requirement for economy in the use of staff, which
is itself an objective of government policy. On top of all this, the
Treasury Minute made it fairly clear that Departments felt that
the report did not take account of evidence given to the PAC.
Other such examples could be cited.

There is perhaps something of a dilemma for the National
Audit Office. If its reports appear too bland, they will not satisfy
the PAC nor the instincts of the new blood among its staff; there
will be cases where something other than blandness is called for
in order to make an impact on institutional defensiveness. There
will also be cases where it is difficult not to observe that the
facilities provided for some activity are inadequate. On the other
hand, the more controversial and open to argument the NAO's
recommendations, the less authoritative they will be, especially if
the findings are felt to be unfair, and the more the NAO will put
itself on a par with a management consultant whose advice one is
free to take or to leave.

However, these are still relatively early days. When the

National Audit Office was set up, it would perhaps have been natural if its first head had felt a need to shed his old civil service coloration and achieve a different public image and a higher profile for the organisation. His relatively recent successor as Comptroller and Auditor General does not have this initial task of putting the National Audit Office on the map, and will no doubt give thought to the possibility of striking a somewhat different balance in resolving his dilemma. On the other hand, the present balance appears to suit the Public Accounts Committee, who probably feel that any disadvantages in the new style of reporting are outweighed by the greater impact that is achieved.

10

The Management of the Civil Service

The last of the questions posed in our third chapter was: how can efficiency and value for money be secured in the management of the non-market services? Simply being in the market sector is no guarantee of efficiency; nevertheless, though market imperfections and protection of one kind and another may blunt the forces of competition, where there is a competitive regime there will be a tendency for poorly managed companies, and even whole industries, to go out of business or to be taken over. Competition and market forces exert pressure to develop good management systems and good managers who will raise profitability and increase market share, and who will cut costs and/or improve or change the product. These pressures are absent in the free or subsidised public services; different pressures and management systems have to be looked for.

There is a tendency to look for similarities between the commercial world and the public services with a view to applying similar management techniques. This approach has some successes to its credit; men and women with a talent for management should be capable of applying it in both spheres, though the skills have not always proved transferable. But the dissimilarities between the market and the non-market sectors are very great.

The absence of the profit and loss criterion is fundamental. Corporate growth, which makes private sector managers tick, and which is accepted as the touchstone of success provided that profits grow too, is the last thing that people want to see from public bodies; in the absence of the profit test, they are conscious only of the cost of growth, even when it is beneficial. There are other things which make public servants tick, as can be seen in the dedication of many of those in medicine or teaching, or in the workaholic lifestyle of the Treasury itself, but no one claims that the public service ethos by itself is a sufficient recipe for cost control and man management.

We need to distinguish between programme expenditure and expenditure on the administration or running of programmes. The 1979 Conservative manifesto aimed to cut both: 'We will scrap expensive Socialist programmes. ... The reduction of waste, bureaucracy and over-government will also yield substantial savings.' Programme expenditure is, in its nature, far larger than administrative or running costs. As an example, the social security benefits paid out in 1988–89 will amount to £48.5 billion. The amount spent by the Department of Social Security, or by local authorities on their behalf, on paying out these benefits will approach £2.4 billion, equal to about 5 per cent of programme expenditure.

Good or bad management can make some difference to the amount spent on programmes; it may make a lot of difference to the value obtained for that money. Nevertheless, the broad magnitude of programme expenditure is determined overwhelmingly by policy decisions and by the circumstances which shape them. In a broad-brush way this is shown by the continuous growth in programme expenditure since 1979, in spite of a more sustained campaign for managerial change in the public services than has ever been seen before. To take a smaller and more particular illustration, if – before the Falklands war – someone had been able to advise effectively against the withdrawal of our one patrol boat from the area, a move interpreted by the Argentine generals as an abandonment of British interest in the islands, he might have saved us more money (as well as a great many lives) than any number of new management methods in the Ministry of Defence. I say this, not to disparage the increased emphasis on management in government affairs in recent years, but as a mild cautionary note against downgrading the importance of good policy advice. However, it is with management, in the sense of managing the government's own manpower, that we are here concerned.

On a recent (1987) count, the numbers in the public services were equivalent to 4.2 million full-time employees. In very round numbers, 2.3 million, including teachers, were employed by local authorities, a million were in the National Health Service and 300,000 in the armed forces. None of these are civil servants, though they are paid for out of public funds and the Treasury are concerned with them to that extent. There are close on 600,000 in the civil service itself, and it is for these, and for some 'fringe bodies' on the periphery of government, that the Treasury and the Cabinet Office have a central management role, though the employing Departments have direct management responsibility. The general observations made in this chapter apply throughout the public services, but the specific problems vary; the rest of this discussion is concerned only with the civil service.

The crudest but most powerful surrogates for market forces in the civil service are cash limits on staff costs and manpower limits or targets. These can hardly be called management systems, but they can put some extra muscle behind such traditional tools of management as staff inspections, performance indicators and performance measurement, and reviews or scrutinies of particular functions. External audit by the National Audit Office is of great value notwithstanding the recent hiccups in its relations with Whitehall; internal audit can also make a contribution.

The blunt instruments of squeeze on money and manpower have the supreme advantage of enabling the central management of the civil service to respond to a political imperative to cut the number of civil servants. They are effective in removing superfluous fat. The danger is that the squeeze will be overdone and the quality of the service will suffer; money and manpower limits are concerned only with inputs, not with outputs. Moreover, though a squeeze on a block budget can force a Department to make choices within the total, there will also be a tendency to achieve cuts unselectively, by a policy of equality of misery across the board, which is often the response to a political imperative. Hence the need to ally the blunt instruments of squeeze with the more selective tools of management.

By a combination of the two approaches, civil service numbers were reduced by 136,500 or 19 per cent between 1978–79 and 1986–87, with some small further reduction still planned. The Treasury could reasonably claim that, where comparisons could be made between roughly comparable types of work in large Departments such as Inland Revenue, Customs and Excise and the DHSS and in large private sector companies such as banks and insurance companies, productivity improvements in the public services had been at least as great as in the private sector. These comparisons could not, however, take account of the quality of service.

This period also saw the birth and growing pains of the Financial Management Initiative. This massive exercise involved, roughly speaking, the setting of objectives and budgets for, usually, middle-ranking civil servants designated as 'cost-centre managers' or 'budget-holders', throughout the service, and the monitoring of performance and output in relation to those objectives and budgets. Top management systems were set up in Departments to give direction to the process. The Management and Personnel Office and the Treasury shared the central responsibility, until the transfer of MPO functions to the Treasury gave it sole responsibility.

The FMI represented the flowering, after a time-lag, of seeds which were sown by Derek Rayner while he was on loan to the government, and which were intended to 'change the culture of Whitehall'. In this it has succeeded to the extent of securing a far greater emphasis in Whitehall on the management role. 'There can be few top civil servants,' writes Sue Richards in *Reshaping Central Government*, 'who do not believe that management is, and more importantly ought to be, a larger part of their workload than it used to be.' I would add, without quarrelling with this, that it should not be imagined that, before the FMI, top civil servants did not bother with management, though they may have called it administration; in very large Departments there was sometimes a division of labour, the Permanent Secretary (or equivalent) concentrating on either administration or policy and relying on his Second Permanent Secretary, or whoever his deputy was, to handle either policy or administration, as the case might be. Nor was it always the case that the top official chose to concentrate on the policy role; for instance, the Chairman of the Board of Inland Revenue did not always prefer the complexities of tax policy to the more human function of dealing with the tax inspectorate and visiting tax offices.

Notwithstanding the impetus behind the FMI, there were limitations on the managerial freedom which budget-holders could be given, especially at the outset. They had no freedom of choice in, for instance, their accommodation or staff numbers or rates of pay. It seemed to me that there was an inherent limitation on the scope for abandoning conventional financial controls without the constraints of profit and loss to replace them. With few exceptions, the FMI involved cost centres rather than profit centres.

No doubt in the business world also many sub-units are cost centres rather than profit centres, but they will normally be subject to the discipline of profit and loss, even if indirectly and as part of a larger unit. Profit centres themselves are unlikely to be wholly free from central controls; these things vary according to the size and style of the company. Even if, say, a subsidiary is given a fairly free hand while it is contributing handsomely to group profits, once it starts losing money group headquarters are bound to intervene. As for cost centres at group headquarters itself, they may have it soft for a time during good spells, but overheads are liable to be slashed during a downturn in profits.

In spite of the inevitable limitations on managerial freedom, after a slow start the view appeared to be gaining ground that the FMI was generally welcomed by civil service managers and had brought about a significant change in attitudes, though it could have little application to smallish groups of staff engaged on policy work. But there were other more critical assessments:

The initiative rests on the belief that by building a better budgetary system, you will get better management. Much activity has gone on in the name of the initiative since its launch in 1982, and many thousands of civil servant hours have been spent in complying with its requirements. In spite of the real improvements which have been made in the quality of management, the ultimate conclusion reached here is that it has been disappointing.

This comes from Sue Richards' contribution to *Reshaping Central Government* (Harrison and Gretton (eds) 1987), which was put together in 1987 at the end of Margaret Thatcher's second term. Later in the same piece Ms Richards writes:

The failure is ascribed to two kinds of factors – the actual process of managing the change, and the inadequacy of the underlying model of management being applied. ... Because of past career-development policies, the current generation of top civil servants has little experience of management to bring to bear on the change process. ... The managerial inexperience of top civil servants also partly explains their willingness to adopt so impoverished a concept of management.

At this point let me interject that top civil servants generally cannot have had much choice in the matter. The passage concludes: 'But it is Thatcherism which is more clearly at the heart of the problem. The very hostility which created the energy to focus on change made change impossible.'

This view was no doubt coloured by the fact that, while the Financial Management Initiative was being introduced, the Treasury still had to deliver its target figure of manpower cuts, which were not always conducive to ideal management and in some cases entailed an acknowledged reduction in standards. Moreover, the manpower targets affected even those services, such as driving tests, which would have been capable of paying for more driving testers out of higher revenue from fees, but which were obliged, instead, to keep the public waiting for tests.

A potentially important change took place in April 1988, when manpower targets for the civil service were discontinued. Staff numbers were still to be monitored, but the essential discipline was now to take the form of limits on running costs, for which a target efficiency gain of 1.5 per cent a year was set; in theory these gains might be applied to either reducing expenditure or to raising output. In general the system of running costs would give

Departments some flexibility between expenditure on manpower and on other administrative costs; but in particular, although these were for the most part to be gross limits, it would be possible for services which could cover their costs from receipts to be exempt from this control. Thus the limit on the number of driving testers would be the number of qualified staff who could be recruited.

Even before this change could come into effect, the *ancien regime* of Whitehall management came under an even more critical assault, this time from within Whitehall, in the shape of a report to the Prime Minister from the Efficiency Unit, called 'Improving Management in Government: The Next Steps.' In many respects the criticisms in this report had much in common with those just quoted although, working to the Prime Minister, the Efficiency Unit, naturally enough, did not direct its attack against Thatcherism. While accepting that 'developments towards more clearly defined and budgeted management are positive and helpful,' the report found that 'senior management is dominated by people whose skills are in policy formulation and who have relatively little experience of managing or working where services are actually being delivered.' In language suggestive of the Red Guards of the Chinese Cultural Revolution, the introduction to the report spoke of 'changing the cultural attitudes and behaviour of government so that continuous improvement becomes a widespread and in-built feature of it'.

The central recommendation of the 'Next Steps' report was that '"agencies" should be established to carry out the executive functions of government within a policy and resources framework set by a department. ... Once the policy objectives and budgets within the framework are set, the management of the agency should then have as much independence as possible in deciding how these objectives are met.'

The work leading up to the report was begun in November 1986 and completed in March 1987, but the report itself was not published until February 1988. We can only speculate about the details of what took place in between. *The Times* reported on 19 February 1988 that 'The Head of the Civil Service, Sir Robin

Butler, denied that there had been "a row" over how much hiving off there should be. But he admitted, in a coded way, that arguments had been fierce.' The reference to hiving off, a phrase which featured a good deal in press reports at the time, illustrates the lack of precision in the report and the extent of the issues which remained to be resolved even after the Prime Minister's announcement on the matter appeared to give 'Next Steps', up to a point, a fair wind.

On the question of hiving off, the report said no more than that 'An "agency" of this kind may be part of government and the civil service, or it may be more effective outside government.' This was a throwback to the Fulton Committee's Report on the Civil Service in 1968 which recommended, among other things, the creation of accountable units of management within Departments and examination of the possibility of a considerable extension of 'hiving off' of autonomous bodies from Departments. There is a great deal of difference between a 'Departmental agency' within a Department, which, like the Department as a whole, comes under the direct authority of a minister who is accountable for it to Parliament, and on the other hand a non-Departmental public body, which comes in the first instance under the authority of a Board or Council or suchlike. Such bodies may be hived off from a government Department – the way in which the Atomic Energy Authority, for instance, and the Civil Aviation Authority came into existence – or they may be created *de novo* like, say, the Scottish Development Agency. In either case, an Act of Parliament is normally required to set up these non-Departmental bodies and to define their powers and those of the minister. The object, in the past, has not normally been simply to delegate executive responsiblity for carrying out government policies but to distance ministers, to a greater or lesser degree, from the policy decisions. In the case of the Arts Council, for instance, or the Research Councils, ministers devolve matters of artistic or scientific judgement to the Councils.

However, there was a backlash against quangos leading to the review of these bodies in 1979 which I mentioned briefly in the opening chapter of this book. The term 'quangos' was then much in use, a popular but misleading acronym for Quasi Autonomous Non-Governmental Bodies, whereas they are an extension of government with a degree of autonomy defined by Act of Parliament. The hostility towards them came from a section of the government's own supporters, which saw in them a creeping extension of government which did not show up in the numbers of civil servants. (For the most part the staffs of these bodies are not part of the Civil Service, but the staff of three bodies hived off from the Department of Employment – the Manpower Services Commission and the Health and Safety Executive in 1974, followed by the Arbitration, Conciliation and Advisory Service in 1976 – retained their civil service status and interchangeability with the Department of Employment itself. The functions of the MSC have now been re-absorbed into the Department.) The critics also saw appointments to quangos as an undesirable form of patronage. The more ideological among them also believed that ministers should be directly accountable to Parliament for all its interventions in the market economy.

The review led to some reduction in the number of these bodies and codified the rules for the remainder. It did not prevent the government from setting up new bodies, such as the Dockland Development Corporation, for particular purposes, but I should have thought that the thinking which led to the review would be an obstacle to the wholesale hiving off of executive functions, as distinct from pursuing the idea of 'Departmental agencies'.

Following the Prime Minister's announcement, it was made known that there was an initial list of a dozen candidates for agency status, including such bodies as the Stationery Office and the Companies Registration Office, which already approximated to agencies but without the degree of independence envisaged in 'Next Steps', and other fairly non-contentious establishments such as the Meteorological Office. A senior official from the Treasury was appointed as a Second Permanent Secretary in the Cabinet Office to take the initiative forward.

An article in the *Observer* on 21 February 1988, under the heading 'Taming the Whitehall Machine', argued that this move 'heralds the most fundamental reform of the civil service this century' and that 'Last Thursday the Prime Minister gave the ratchet of Thatcherism another decisive twist.' On the other hand, the initial report in *The Times* on 19 February 1988 took the view that 'Treasury officials ... have won a large victory after eight months of infighting' and that they 'would retain tight control of the agencies and how much their chief executives and staff were paid.'

I doubt whether the Treasury saw this as primarily a matter of Whitehall power politics or whether they had any hostility to the concept of agencies. They would, I think, have been greatly concerned with the problem of reconciling this concept with the Treasury's responsibilities for public service pay and manpower and public expenditure generally. I should myself expect some inherent constraints to remain in the era of agencies just as there had been limitations to the Financial Management Initiative. I do not imagine, either, that other Departments looked on with detachment as the issue was contested between the Efficiency Unit and the Treasury. Some, I dare say, would welcome the idea of agencies more than others, but all of them would be concerned with the practicalities of how far the idea could be applied and how it could be made to work.

11

Privatisation

'The balance of our society has been increasingly tilted in favour of the State,' wrote Margaret Thatcher in her Foreword to the 1979 Conservative election manifesto,' ... we have to reverse that process.'

The success of the privatisation programme has been an enormous bonus to the Conservative government in pursuing that aim. Whereas its original targets for public expenditure and the money supply were not achieved, the disposal of publicly owned industries has gone farther and faster than was ever foreseen at the outset; this did much to reconcile the right wing of the party to the compromises on public expenditure.

Privatisation did not feature prominently in the 1979 manifesto, which undertook only 'to sell back to private ownership the recently nationalised aerospace and shipbuilding concerns, ... to sell shares in the National Freight Corporation,' and to sell off 'as circumstances permit' the temporary shareholdings administered by the National Enterprise Board. But after the success of the initial share flotations, the programme of disposals acquired momentum, especially in the government's second term. By the end of 1987 the list of disposals included, on top of those proposed in the manifesto, such major enterprises as British Airways, Britoil and Cable and Wireless, and two giant organisations – British Gas and British Telecommunications. In 1986–87 privatisation proceeds rose to £4.4 billion and were expected to run at around £5 billion in each of the next four years.

While they were in public ownership, most of these

enterprises had been, not companies with a share capital, but public corporations with no share capital and no shareholders. They were run by Boards appointed by ministers, who had various powers in relation to the Boards but, technically, the government did not 'own' these industries. Nor, in any meaningful sense, did the public. The assets were vested by law in the Boards themselves. Paternity for this form of public ownership is generally credited to Herbert Morrison, Lord President of the Council in the 1945 Labour government, who co-ordinated the programme of nationalisation and who took as his model the London Passenger Transport Board which he had created when Minister of Transport in a pre-war Labour government.

Since it was not possible to sell shares in these public corporations as they stood, it was necessary to take powers in each case to set up a company to which the assets of the corporation could be transferred, and then to offer shares in the new company for sale. This technique was first devised in the summer of 1979, in an exercise in which I was involved in my last months at the Department of Trade, with a view to privatising British Airways. This plan went beyond the manifesto and was received with acclaim by the government's supporters, but the intended flotation of British Airways shares was delayed, first, by a slump in the profitability of airlines generally, and then because of litigation resulting from the collapse of Laker Airways, which complained of a conspiracy against it by other airlines. However, the technique worked out for that project was adopted for all the privatisation issues which did take place.

The objective of raising money for the Exchequer by these disposals, which later became an important by-product of the privatisation programme, played no part in the Conservatives' hostility to nationalisation, and little or no part in the gathering impetus of its drive for privatisation. A minor illustration of this was provided by the privatisation of the National Freight Corporation; after providing money to put the Company's pension fund in good shape, the government received no net proceeds from the sale of shares in the company, now renamed the National Freight Consortium; this operation was exceptional in that the management and the employees acquired shareholding control and turned the company into a highly profitable enterprise, greatly enhancing the value of their shareholdings.

The prime motives for privatisation were, not Exchequer gain, but an ideological belief in free markets and a wider distribution of private ownership of property, not common ownership: there was also a belief that the monolithic public corporations and their monolithic trade unions had played a large part in wage inflation, and a conviction that no commercial organisation can be fully efficient if the government is involved in it. Any notion that the mere fact of public ownership is bound to lead to inefficiency is belied, it seems to me, by the performance of British Petroleum when its shares were largely owned by the government, but the management of BP were allowed to run it as a commercial company, not a public corporation. It is a matter of history, which I have spelled out in detail elsewhere, that neither Labour nor Conservative governments had been able to refrain from intervention in the running of the nationalised industries or to devise a durable regime which satisfied both their own policy requirements and the aspirations of the boards to manage their enterprises.

For the new government to give this as a reason for privatisation was a curious admission, even a protestation, of its own inability to manage the relationship any better; but certainly, to the managements of the nationalised industries, the new constraints of the PSBR must have seemed only one more twist of the screw, though perhaps a different screw, now that they were obliged to raise prices and their rate of return on capital, from the period when they had been forced to depress prices and run deficits in pursuit of the price restraint policies of Edward Heath's Conservative government.

The interesting thing is that, after the furious debates about public ownership in earlier decades, the political opposition to privatisation crumbled fairly quickly and the expected trade union opposition largely failed to materialise. A large part of the nationalised sector of industry had come about for organisational rather than ideological reasons, through bringing together on a national scale public utilities which had begun life at municipal

level, or through hiving off public corporations such as the Post
Office or the British Airports Authority which had previously
been run as government Departments or parts of government
Departments; while Rolls Royce and British Leyland, having run
into financial trouble, were acquired as rescue operations by
Edward Heath's Conservative government and Harold Wilson's
Labour government respectively. But it was an ideological
commitment to common ownership which led to the great wave
of nationalisation under the first post-war Labour government.
A number of philosophical strands came together in this
commitment; among them, and stemming from the miseries of
the industrial revolution and after, was a belief that, since wealth
and privilege went with the ownership of land and industry, the
many who owned nothing would benefit from wider ownership.

It seems unlikely that much of this belief can have survived.
The post-war rise in living standards of working people, making
possible personal ownership of homes and cars for the better off
among them, was due to technological change and economic
growth generally. Some of the nationalised industries made
important contributions to this growth, but other countries with
less public ownership could be seen to be growing more rapidly.
In any event, the impersonal public corporations did not give the
public any sense of ownership. Even among the leadership of the
Labour Party there appeared to be some disenchantment with
that form of public ownership.

As for the top management of the nationalised industries, their
main concern was to ensure that their enterprises, if privatised,
would be sold as a single entity, in each case, and not broken up
into a number of separate companies. Once assured on this point,
they had no reason to make difficulties, which in any event
would have been unlikely to deter the government, and in fact
they had good reason to look forward to freedom from political
control. British Airways also sought, and obtained, an assurance
that it would retain intact its rights to fly on its existing routes –
an invaluable asset, since passenger airlines are not allowed to
operate internationally except on routes agreed between the
governments concerned; it was believed that this assurance
would also go far to carry the workforce with the privatisation

exercise. No doubt the avoidance of a break-up was important to the employees of other nationalised industries also.

The privatisation of British Telecommunications and British Gas as single entities came under criticism, principally but not exclusively from the New Right, as replacing state-owned monopolies by privately owned monopolies; similar complaints were made of the disposal of British Airways which, though it has to compete internationally with all the rest of the world's great airlines, has little effective competition on international routes from other British airlines. The critics have not been appeased by the setting up of Oftel and Ofgas as watchdog bodies, but British Telecommunications and British Gas themselves do not regard these as toothless creatures; British Airways remain under the supervision of the Civil Aviation Authority, which has a long-standing responsibility for regulating British airlines generally. In its preparations for the privatisation of the electricity supply industry, the Department of Energy, seeking to avoid the criticisms made of the lack of competition in telecommunications and gas supply, and in the face of some hostility from within the industry, has gone to some lengths to introduce an element of competition into the planned structure for electricity generation; so far this move does not seem to have carried much conviction, but the Secretary of State for Energy, Mr Parkinson, has spoken in bullish terms of the prospect of entrepreneurs queuing up to provide new generating capacity.

Against this political background, the positive reason why the privatisation issues went well was quite simply that shares in major companies with great potential were being offered at favourable prices – to judge by the fact that in most cases the issues were over-subscribed and share allotments had to be rationed – and that the shares immediately went to a premium in market trading and could be resold at a profit by those buyers (a high proportion of the total) who wanted to make short-term gains. For the small and the first-time investor there was the further attraction that share applications could be made without going through a stockbroker or paying any transaction fees, as is the case with normal share purchases. A whole new class of investors was introduced to the pleasures of dabbling in the stock market and making money without actually working.

The successful privatisation of British Telecommunications was a great leap forward in this process. It was by far the biggest operation up to that date, even though only a majority of the shares were offered for sale at that stage, the remainer being retained by the government for later disposal. New ground was broken in the techniques of expensive publicity and mass marketing of shares. A precedent was set for the privatisation of a monopoly industry. The government was emboldened to enlarge the scale of its thinking about future privatisation. It became apparent that, given time, very little, if anything, would be left of the nationalised sector.

The Treasury has throughout played a co-ordinating role in the programme, at both ministerial and official level. The sponsor Department dealing with the affairs of each nationalised industry is in the lead in the privatisation of that industry, but the Treasury division which has a longstanding central responsibility for general policy on the nationalised industries has taken on a similar central function in the privatisation programme. It also takes part in the planning of each operation and has by now become a repository of expertise in this field. In cases where only a part of the share capital of a privatised company is offered for sale initially, the Treasury has become custodian of the remaining shares and is then in the lead on any 'secondary sale' of this shareholding.

After the partly-paid price of the British Telecommunications shares had nearly doubled overnight, there was a general expectation among the investing public that there would be a profit to be made on all subsequent privatisation issues. So great was this confidence that otherwise respectable members of society were prepared to break the law by making multiple applications for privatisation shares in order to make multiple profits on their resale. This mood of optimism was encouraged by a sustained bull market in company shares generally and the steep rise in average share prices until they reached a peak in 1987.

No doubt it is not always easy to judge beforehand the exact price which will maximise the proceeds of a particular share issue. Let us take as an example the offer for sale of British Airways shares at 125p a share, of which 65p was payable on application and the balance later. We find from a report by the National Audit Office, who will have had access to all the papers of the Department of Transport – now the Department responsible for civil aviation – that the Department's advisers considered that a price of 130p, only 5p higher, 'could lead to a failure of the issue'. In fact, at 125p the public offer was subscribed 32 times over; at the end of the first day's trading the partly paid (65p) shares stood at 109p, a premium of 44p. In retrospect it seems most unlikely that another 5p on the price would have led to a failure of the issue, but professional advisers are no doubt bound to give cautious counsel, and the government, with a whole series of flotations in prospect, and unwilling to jeopardise them by breaking the run of successes, is no doubt bound to play safe in such a situation.

The sales literature for each flotation included a warning that share prices can go down as well as up. In the heyday of the bull market this may have seemed a purely ritual form of words, but the risk suddenly became reality when a crash in share prices began on the New York stock exchange one Friday in October, continuing after the weekend on Black Monday, 19 October 1987, when the Dow Jones index fell further by over 22 per cent, a worse fall in a single day than had occurred even during the disastrous Wall Street crash of 1929. Panic selling spread immediately to all the world's stock exchanges. In London the Financial Times share index fell by over 10 per cent on the Monday and 22 per cent during the week.

This time the Treasury's luck ran out. After its offer of 31.7 per cent of the shares in British Petroleum had been underwritten, but before the closing date for applications, the market price of BP shares already in circulation plunged below the price at which the Treasury holding had been put on sale; obviously there were no takers at that price (when anybody could buy BP shares already on the market more cheaply), apart from 270,000 investors who had taken up the Treasury offer before the crash. The rest of the issue was left with the underwriters, who would have to take a loss on reselling the shares. The Chancellor of the Exchequer offered to buy shares back, through the Bank of England, at a floor price of 70p which, though far below the 120p paid by purchasers as the first instalment of the sale price, would limit the potential losses of investors and underwriters. In the event, most of the issue was resold on the market, rather than to the Bank of England, somewhat above this floor price. One paradoxical result of the operation was that the British government was replaced as a major shareholder in BP by the government of Kuwait, through the Kuwait Investment Office, which took up a substantial part of the shares put on the market. Few tears were shed for the British underwriters, who had received substantial fees from previous privatisation issues, and who had off-loaded much of their risk from the BP sale to a large number of sub-under-writers, but underwriters in the United States, Canada and Japan, who carried most of the risk themselves, had their fingers burned.

This setback did not deter the Treasury from its plans to continue the privatisation programme in 1988. Unlike the Wall Street crash of 1929, the fall in share prices in 1987 had not so far been accompanied by a recession in the real economy, and could be disregarded as no more than the reversal of an excessive rise in the final phase of the bull market. There appeared still to be plenty of money around for investment in further privatisation issues and still a good deal of interest in them in the market.

Although the motivation of the programme was political, the Treasury was not at all indifferent to its financial advantages to the Exchequer. Selling the family silver played an increasingly useful part in reducing the Public Sector Borrowing Requirement and making room for limited tax reductions in the latter part of the government's second term, though the Chancellor claimed – and events bore this out – that these proceeds did no more than bring the reductions forward in time.

One of the oddities of the privatisation programme has been the hankering to treat the proceeds, not as a receipt, which they palpably are, but as negative expenditure, reducing the public expenditure total. This affects two different public expenditure aggregates which are used in different contexts. As already noted in chapter 4, the Treasury's graphs of general government expenditure as a percentage of GDP show two profiles tracing the rise and fall of this aggregate: the upper profile has the caption 'Excluding privatisation proceeds', while the lower profile, uncaptioned, by implication includes these proceeds as a negative expenditure item. However, more emphasis is now placed, rightly, on the upper line, perhaps reflecting a feeling that it is no longer quite so important politically to treat privatisation as a substitute for public expenditure cuts, and also a growing confidence that the objective of reducing public expenditure as a percentage of GDP can be achieved without bringing privatisation receipts into the reckoning. However, in the planning total – an aggregate which has been explained in chapter 5 – privatisation proceeds were still listed in the 1988 public expenditure White Paper as a minus item, thus reducing the total. But whether these sums are treated as increasing government receipts or as reducing government expenditure, their real effect is the same.

In terms of promoting wider share ownership, privatisation has been a remarkable success. 'Survey evidence suggests that at the beginning of 1987 there were 8½ million adult shareholders, treble the number in 1979,' states the public expenditure White Paper. (By the beginning of 1988, in spite of the stock market fall which had occurred, this number had risen to 9 million.) This refers to the number of shareholders in all companies. The number in privatised companies at that date would have gone far to account for this increase. At a somewhat later date, after those who bought shares only to resell them had dropped out, the number remaining on the share registers of the privatised companies was put at over 5.5 million.

In all the major flotations employees were given a number of free shares and offered free shares to match any which they bought or shares at a discount, up to a limit. The great majority of employees took advantage of these concessions. The wide take-up of shares presented the Labour party with new problems. The situation was in sharp contrast to the 1950s, when Labour's threat to re-nationalise the privatised steel companies was an effective discouragement to investment in the industry. Now, proposals for re-nationalisation at no more than the original issue price failed to carry conviction and were rejected at the Labour Party conference in Brighton in October 1987. Before the 1987 stock market crash such terms would have deprived investors, including employees and other small shareholders, of the capital appreciation to that date, and even after the fall in share prices would in most cases have failed to compensate them for the value of their shares. The effect of subsequent fluctuations in share prices was of course unpredictable, but the popularity of privatisation shares appeared to confirm the appeal of private ownership and suggested the need for fresh thinking about nationalisation as a major plank in Labour's programme. But the same gathering at Brighton passed a motion calling for a statement on the extension of *social* ownership to be presented to the following year's conference, leaving it in doubt whether the party's leaders could carry the party with them in more than a change in terminology, or at most in the forms of public ownership.

Wider share ownership did not mean control by the small man, still less by the workforce, with the notable exception of the National Freight Consortium. The maximum value of the inducements to employees to become shareholders had not exceeded £600 per head; this could help employees to get a stake in their company which had not been possible under the public corporation regime, but the resulting shareholdings added up to only a tiny fraction of the share capital of the massive privatised companies.

Nor did privatisation do anything to reverse or halt the trend towards an increased concentration of share ownership in the hands of institutions such as insurance companies, pension funds and investment trusts, who now hold a majority of all the shares in UK quoted companies, while individuals hold only a minority. According to a survey of privatisation in *The Observer* of 25 October 1987, 'Between 1963 and 1981 the proportion of the stock market directly owned by individuals fell from 54 per cent to 28 per cent. Statistics available for 1986 indicate that out of a total equity market valued at £368 billion, some £88 billion was owned by individuals, or 24 per cent.'

The privatised sector generally conforms closely to this pattern. Inspection of the 'shareholder profiles' for a number of major privatised companies shows that, notwithstanding a very large number of small shareholders – literally millions in the case of the two giants, British Telecommunications and British Gas – the majority of the shares are held by a much smaller number of institutional and corporate investors. At the same time, the shares are sufficiently spread among these larger shareholders – each of them having only a small percentage, say 2 or 3 per cent, of the total issued share capital – as to avoid giving a potentially dominant position to any one of them or even any group of them. (The Kuwaiti holding of over 20 per cent in BP is a special case.)

For any company in this situation, the managerial revolution – the divorce of management from ownership – has become a reality. The Board takes its own decisions, within the constraints of the law and the market, and chooses its own membership and its successors (subject to the formality of confirmation by an Annual General Meeting of the shareholders) without any outside intervention so long as it can pay satisfactory dividends and avoids being taken over by a predator. For companies in a competitive industry, profitability cannot be taken for granted and the risk of being taken over is real; but the privatised utilities have sheltered markets, and both they and others among the privatised companies have been given special protection against takeover, by means of a provision in their Articles of Association which limits any single shareholding to 15 per cent of the total issued share capital; in some of these cases the government retains a golden share which would enable it to prevent a change in this restriction in the Articles of Association; both of these precautions have been built into the arrangements for British Gas, British Telecommunications and some of the others. The Articles of Association of British Airways provide powers to put a limit of 15 per cent on any individual shareholding and a limit of 25 per cent on total foreign shareholdings; these powers can be exercised only if the Secretary of State for Transport considers it necessary to use them in order to protect BA against the loss of routes which could result from its ceasing to be recognised by the governments concerned as a British airline for the purposes of international air services agreements.

Like the rest of the private sector, the privatised companies are now free from Whitehall control. They no longer have to negotiate their investment plans with government officials. Their pricing policies may be subject to regulation but not to ministerial pressure. They can make acquisitions, and they have begun to expand into new activities in the UK and, up to a point, abroad. They can reward their employees, and the Directors, in line with the benefits, including stock options, prevailing in the corporate world.

On top of these normal private sector freedoms, many of the privatised companies enjoy, as we have just noted, a preferential position through a near-monopoly or immunity to take-over or both. Nevertheless they give every indication of having the same concern with shareholder relations and their ranking with the investor community as other major companies. It is natural, therefore, to ask whether this creates a risk that, in the near-monopoly industries, the interests of users may be subordinated to these concerns. Considerable attention, therefore, is now focused on the performance of the regulatory bodies. The question is whether systematised regulation of privately owned monopolies can deliver a better deal for the user than overlordship of state monopolies by ministers and officials. It is probably too early to pass judgment on this, but the regulated companies do not expect that we shall see 'regulator capture' here such as is said to have occurred sometimes in the United States, while the regulators themselves sound confident.

12

Monetary Policy and the MTFS –
the First Term

In the period after 1979, Britain's economic and financial affairs were dominated by monetary doctrines which had gained acceptance among a group of leading Conservative policy-makers while they were in the wilderness after Edward Heath had made way for the Labour administrations of Harold Wilson and James Callaghan. There was a great deal of soul-searching then to find a way of running things which would be different from that of all three of those Prime Ministers.

A major difference in the new approach has been the rejection of neo-Keynesian policies of demand management designed to achieve or maintain full employment, policies which led to rising budget deficits and public borrowing. Let me quote from a paper by Sir Terence Burns, the Treasury's Chief Economic Adviser:

> Although apparently successful at first, this strategy increasingly came under question as it became associated with a steady acceleration of inflation after 1961. ... The growth of money GDP (GDP expressed in current prices) increased from an average of 7 per cent per annum in the economic cycle from 1961 to 1965 to almost 18 per cent in the cycle from 1973 to 1979. Extra output accounted for almost half the increase in money GDP from 1961 to 1965, but by 1973–79 real output growth accounted for less than one-tenth of the increase.

He goes on to say that 'The Medium Term Financial Strategy (MTFS) was introduced in 1980 with the objective of reversing these trends.' In this and the following chapter I attempt to trace how the MTFS has evolved.

The Treasury, though sensitive to any suggestion of a change of policy, acknowledges that there have been some changes in the MTFS. It may be a matter of emphasis whether you stress the changes or the continuity. Let me quote Terry Burns again:

> The MTFS . . . as it continues to be pursued today, is identifiably the same as at the outset. It has clearly evolved both in presentation and substance, most particularly in the technicalities of the assessment of monetary conditions. It would have been surprising if there had not been changes. But the strategy remains very much intact – the commitment to a nominal framework; the medium-term horizon; elimination of high levels of public sector borrowing; and the prominent role of monetary policy.

Certainly the priority given to reducing inflation, not intermittently but over a sequence of years, has remained virtually intact. So too has the primacy of the instruments of fiscal policy – specifically a reduction in public borrowing – and interest rates. Changes which have taken place in the MTFS in other respects are seen, from a Treasury perspective, as changes in emphasis only or in intermediate objectives, not affecting the overall strategy, and as the correct response to developments in the economy and in financial institutions. However, to the less committed this can seem to be playing down too far the changes in the way that the MTFS has been expressed.

By this I do not mean simply that the initial monetary targets were not hit or that the definitions of the targets have been changed. It was recognised from the outset that the definition then chosen 'may need to be adjusted from time to time'; the instruments which serve as money themselves undergo change – for instance, building society deposits have acquired new uses as the building societies have taken on more and more banking functions – and the way in which monetary policy is operated must respond to changes in the financial system. (At the same time, the substitution of new targets for old has surely gone further than the 'adjustments' foreseen at the outset.) Nor do I have principally in mind the fact that the exchange rate, which did not feature at all in the original version of the MTFS, has a crucial role in the latest version, while exchange rate policy itself has moved from benign neglect to the active pursuit of exchange rate stability – an objective which has been made feasible, in the Treasury's eyes, by the worldwide convergence of inflation at low rates, whereas it could not have been contemplated in the early 1980s.

But there has been a noteworthy change, as I see it, in the theory of the MTFS – whatever effect the change had on monetary policy in practice – in that, at the very beginning, the Chancellor and at least some of his circle appear to have believed that they could *control* the stock or supply of money, and that this was the mechanism which would squeeze out inflation; whereas money supply figures later came to be seen as *indicators* to help in interpreting monetary conditions, which the authorities seek to influence rather than literally to control. Reducing the growth of the money *stock* has been displaced as a central concept by the objective of reducing the growth of money GDP, i.e. the total flow of money *expenditure,* and improving the division of higher money GDP between higher real output and higher prices – more growth in output and less inflation – an objective with which I should think it hard to quarrel.

It is possible that a belief in the ability of the authorities literally to control the money supply, and in the unique importance of a single target for growth in the money supply, did not last long, perhaps less than the first year of the MTFS. If that is so, there appears to have been a time-lag before the conversion was fully reflected in the presentation of the MTFS. There were no doubt political inhibitions on too rapid or too overt a change in its presentation, inhibitions which would tend to be eased later on as the government could claim growing success in the reduction of inflation. Some of the other presentational changes from year to year no doubt reflected a genuine and continuing learning curve in the art of monitoring and interpreting monetary conditions.

To illustrate how thinking has developed, we need to start at the beginning and work our way through. To begin with definitions, all measures of the supply or stock of money include 'the pound in your pocket', in Harold Wilson's classic phrase, whether notes or coin, and also notes and coin in the banks. But most money nowadays is not in the form of cash but of deposits in bank accounts, whether current accounts which have usually been non-interest-bearing, though some current accounts do now pay interest, or interest-bearing accounts of various kinds. Different monetary aggregates, or measures of the money supply, include a greater or lesser part of total bank deposits, on top of notes and coin.

A summary of the definitions employed in the early days of the MTFS is to be found in the following extract from an article headed *WHAT IS MONEY?* from the July 1980 issue of the Treasury's Economic Progress Report:

> The precise definitions of the measures used in the UK are:
>
> M1: a narrow measure consisting of notes and coin in circulation with the public plus sterling sight deposits held by the UK private sector.
> Sterling M3 (£M3): comprising notes and coin in circulation with the public, together with all sterling deposits (including certificates of deposit) held by UK residents in both public and private sectors.
> M3: equalling £M3 plus all bank deposits held by UK residents in other currencies.
>
> In all three definitions, deposits are confined only to those with institutions included in the UK banking sector. The Bank of England also publishes figures showing the private sector's holdings of liquid assets (including building societies' deposits) outside these measures of money

Let us jump to April 1988 and a useful up-to-date list of the main monetary aggregates set out in an article on *Broad money and inflation* in that month's Economic Progress Report. The most notable changes from 1980 are the prominence given to MO (which equates with what is known as the monetary base) and the disappearance of M1 which, as will be seen as the narrative develops, once loomed so large, but which is now treated as a component of M3:

MAIN MONETARY AGGREGATES

Narrow Money

'Narrow money' refers to money balances which are readily available to finance current spending, that is to say for 'transactions purposes'.

M0

Notes and coin in circulation with the public
    plus banks' till money
    plus banks' operational balances with the Bank of England.

Broad money

'Broad money' refers to money held for transactions purposes and money held as a form of saving. It provides an indicator of the private sector's holdings of relatively liquid assets – assets which could be converted with relative ease and without capital loss into spending on goods and services.

M3

Notes and coin in circulation with the public
    plus private sector sterling sight bank deposits
    plus private sector sterling time bank deposits
    plus private sector holdings of sterling bank certificates of deposit.

M4

M3
    plus private sector holdings of building society shares and deposits and sterling certificates of deposit
    minus building society holdings of bank deposits and bank certificates of deposit, and notes and coin.

M5

M4
    plus holdings by the private sector (excluding building societies) of money market instruments (bank bills, Treasury bills, local authority deposits), certificates of tax deposit and national savings instruments (excluding certificates, SAYE and other long-term deposits).

We need to distinguish between money, whichever of the aggregates we use, and credit. In monetary theory, credit is not the same thing as money. 'Money is used to pay bills; credit is used to delay paying them,' writes Alan Walters in *Britain's Economic Renaissance* (1986). Nevertheless, bank deposits are matched by bank loans 'the credit counterparts of the money stock', in the words of a Green Paper on Monetary Control in March 1980 – and bank loans are the principal means of creating money and increasing the money supply. For many years governments used controls on credit as a means of limiting the creation of money.

From definitions of the money supply we can move on to targets for the growth of the money supply. Such targets were first published in Britain when Denis Healey was Chancellor of the Exchequer in the last Labour government; the Treasury and the Bank of England had been framing money supply targets for several years before that, but had not been publishing them. Denis Healey is therefore sometimes credited with introducing monetarism into government policy; Alan Walters has written that 'In 1975–76, for example, Britain witnessed the development of monetary targets and the eschewing of finely tuned fiscality. The Medium Term Financial Strategy of the government of Mrs Thatcher was a lineal descendant of these brave measures of Mr Healey.' (1986)

To ascribe paternity for the MTFS to Denis Healey seems to me to be going too far. He was described at the time as an unbelieving monetarist, meaning that he adopted monetary targets only with a view to inspiring confidence in the financial world which *did* believe in them. It is true that he was keenly aware of the constraints imposed on the government's room for manoeuvre by the need for such confidence, at home and internationally – something which is now more generally recognised than it used to be. In a lecture to the Council for Foreign Affairs in Washington in October 1979, shortly after he left office, he said: 'A government takes great risks when it flies in the face of market opinion . . . however misguided that opinion may be.'

Yet he did also attach importance to monetary policy in its

own right, although with some agnosticism about the practicalities. Later in the same lecture he said:

> Almost the only uncontroversial statement about money supply is one on which Keynes and Friedman would agree: "No continued and substantial inflation can occur without monetary growth that substantially exceeds the rate of real growth." We can all say yes to that. And I think most people would agree that if monetary growth exceeds the rate of real growth as much as it did for two years under my predecessor, Lord Barber, galloping inflation is bound to follow. But beyond that, all is uncertain. We do not know how monetary growth influences inflation, or with what time-lag. We do not know how to measure the relevant monetary growth or how best to influence it. And some economists still believe that changes in the velocity of circulation may make monetary growth an unreliable indicator in any case.

And later still in the lecture we find: 'All this is not to argue against the necessity for controlling monetary growth. . . . It is to argue for a more skeptical and pragmatic approach than is now in vogue . . . '.

In contrast, the Conservative government's Medium Term Financial Strategy was inspired by *believing* monetarists. It was unveiled in the Red Book, the traditional Financial Statement and Budget Report, which was presented to the House of Commons at the time of the 1980 Budget, and which stated categorically that 'Control of the money supply will over a period of years reduce the rate of inflation.' The centrepiece of the strategy was a target range which showed the growth of M3 (or, strictly speaking, Sterling £M3, which excludes non-sterling deposits) reducing from 7–11 per cent in 1980–81 to 6–8 per cent in 1983–84.

How was this to be achieved, against a background of rising inflation, for which previous governments had failed to find a durable remedy? The strategy relied on two instruments only. One was a progressive reduction in the Public Sector Borrowing Requirement, the PSBR for short, which includes the borrowings not only of the central government but also of the local authorities and the public corporations. In order to achieve this, public spending would be cut: 'A key element in the strategy is a reduction in public expenditure.' It is interesting that special sales of assets played little part in the supporting projections of public expenditure, which illustrates that privatisation did not loom large in the government's plans at that stage. The Red Book also held out a conditional expectation of tax reductions. We have already seen that public expenditure – 'a key element in the strategy' – did not, in the event, come down. Nor, as we shall see, did taxation. But the PSBR, after a hiccup, did.

The PSBR, an aggregate peculiar to the UK, is the crucial link between monetary policy and fiscal (or budgetary) policy, since any deficit in the central government budget, plus any money raised and on-lent from the Treasury's National Loans Fund to local authorities and public corporations, has to be financed by government borrowing. (This statement excludes, for simplicity, borrowings by the local authorities and public corporations direct from the market, which also come within the Treasury's definition of the PSBR. On the other hand, the definition excludes borrowings by the Treasury's Exchange Equalisation Account to finance its intervention in foreign exchange markets and other operations.)

To the extent that these borrowings are effected from the banking system (rather than by sales of government securities outside the banking system) the money lent by the banks, like other bank lending, will increase the money supply. Even when the government's borrowing requirements are financed outside the banking system, if they are on a large scale they will tend to push up interest rates. Over time they will add up to a large national debt with a growing burden of debt interest. It is also argued that they will 'crowd out' private borrowing and investment. Conversely, a low PSBR will make it less difficult to regulate the money supply as a whole without excessive interest rates and, it is argued, will be helpful to confidence and diminish inflationary expectations. The promotion of confidence, and making a clean break with the inflationary psychology of the recent past, were principal objectives of the commitment to the MTFS.

Interest rates were to be the other essential instrument of

monetary control, and the only instrument directly affecting the creation of money by bank lending to the private sector. The Green Paper on Monetary Control had discussed, and rejected, other possible instruments, including quantitative ceilings on bank lending which had been in force up to 1971. To a born-again monetarist such a scheme does not qualify as a control on *money*, but in any event it is arguable – though this argument was not used in the Green Paper – that the re-introduction of such a control would not work now that exchange control has been discontinued; the control would not bite on money borrowed from overseas lenders.

At the time of the Green Paper there was in operation a quantitative control (popularly known as 'the corset') on bank deposits defined as 'interest-bearing eligible liabilities' (IBELS). (Deposits appear on the liabilities side of a bank's balance sheet, because the money belongs to the customer, and can be withdrawn by him. Loans appear on the assets side, because the money belongs to the bank, and must be repaid to it with interest.) Under this scheme, a bank was penalised (through having to place special supplementary deposits with the Bank of England) if its IBELS grew more than was allowed. One result of this squeeze on the banking system was that certain transactions were forced outside the banking system, especially 'by the build-up of the so-called bill leak', as the Green Paper put it, and it was decided to discontinue this control.

For that matter, the Green Paper observed that 'In the real world, there are no techniques of monetary control which involve no risk of disintermediation' – that is, of evasion by means of transactions outside the scope of the control. Thus the whole weight of the strategy, in relation to the private sector, would be placed on interest rates, which the government would have to be prepared to raise to unpredictable levels.

For the sake of completeness, mention should also be made of two other types of operation, apart from interest rates, which may be classed as instruments of monetary policy. One of these is intervention in the foreign exchange market by trading sterling for foreign currencies and vice versa; this can influence the exchange rate, which in turn affects costs and prices. The other is 'funding policy', which normally refers to policy on funding the government's borrowing requirements through sales of government securities outside the banking system; this has already been discussed a few paragraphs back. There was, however, a phase in the early 1980s when the Treasury and the Bank of England operated a policy of 'overfunding the PSBR', that is, selling more government securities to the investing public than was necessary in order to meet the government's own requirements. This was done in order to divert money from bank deposits and so to reduce M3, which was then thought too high. However, that resulted in a shortage of liquid funds available to business and industry, which the authorities sought to remedy by buying up commercial bills and thus acquiring a 'bill mountain'. This policy was unwound in due course and is now generally regarded – perhaps even in the Treasury – as having been an aberration. Having mentioned these other instruments of monetary policy, we can now restate that, for practical purposes, the weight of day-to-day monetary policy has rested heavily on interest rates.

The Green Paper also concluded that 'targets are best set in terms of a single aggregate', and that this aggregate should be M3, which had been chosen for the Healey targets and was 'well understood in the markets'. At the same time, the Green Paper stated that the definition might need to be adjusted from time to time, and that the government would take account of the growth of other aggregates. It is interesting that the exchange rate was not mentioned as one of these, though it later came to occupy a prominent place in the strategy.

At the time I wondered why it should be believed that the MTFS would succeed when previous plans, in particular Harold Wilson's National Plan and Edward Heath's plans to regenerate British industry, had gone off course, and both statutory and voluntary incomes policies had broken down in the end – from all of which I tended towards the view that there is an inherent tendency for government plans to go wrong. The answer given to me by some influential monetarists was that this time the government would control the one thing which could be controlled, and this was, astonishingly, the money supply.

The Chancellor used similar language, but taking in more than just the money supply, when he said that the MTFS was 'concerned with only those things that the government had it in their power to control'. Alan Walters wrote later that the MTFS 'gave a coherence to all the financial aspects of policy. And it concentrated on those elements of the financial system over which the government had considerable control – as distinct from many previous "national plans" which dealt with concepts far beyond the reach of government fiat.' (1986)

My pessimism about government plans, esecially the plans of new governments, appeared, at first blush, to be borne out by events. In the course of the first year of the MTFS, every figure in it which was planned to come down failed to do so, but on the contrary went up. M3 grew by 20 per cent from February 1980 to February 1981, as compared with its target range of 7–11 per cent. The abolition of the corset, and the consequent re-entry into the banking system (or 'reintermediation') of transactions which had been squeezed outside it, contributed to the increase but is not thought to have accounted for the bulk of it. This was a very difficult phase in the learning curve.

Interest rates went up to a peak of 17 per cent in the summer of 1980 but the rate of inflation also reached a peak of over 21 per cent. The exchange rate also rose strongly and was to reach a peak of $2.40. Unemployment rose above 2 million during the year and was eventually to go above 3 million. Taxation (taken together with national insurance contributions, which have much the same effect on take-home pay) was going up; with the revenue base depressed by falling national output, and with unemployment benefit contributing to an increase in public expenditure, the PSBR in 1980–81 exceeded the budgeted £8.5 billion by an amount close to £5 billion.

Squeezed by the combination of slump and rising costs, and rendered uncompetitive internationally by the exchange rate, much of British industry was in great distress. (The exceptions included oil companies, who do well when the oil price rises and are in trouble when it falls, and those companies for whom the principal effect of the high exchange rate was a saving on the sterling cost of imported raw materials.) While the Bank of

England, in one capacity, was dutifully pushing up interest rates, in another capacity it was occupied in organising financial support to help deserving companies weather the storm. Donald MacDougall, formerly Chief Economic Adviser in the Treasury, and at that time performing a similar role at the Confederation of British Industry, has written in his memoirs (*Don and Mandarin*, 1987) that for all their political support for the Conservative government, the more sophisticated members of the CBI

> began to question whether the Government was not making a grave mistake, and causing irreparable damage to the economy, by relying so much on trying to control a particular monetary aggregate (Sterling M3). Though this was rising faster than the Government's target, there were no signs in the real world of the sort of things supposed to result from an excessive money supply: rising property prices, a consumer boom, a weakening exchange rate, accelerating inflation, falling unemployment, supply shortages. At least by the autumn of 1980 – little more than a year after the Government took office – these indicators were all pointing in the opposite direction, not at overheating, but an exceedingly contractionary situation; with property markets stagnant, consumers' expenditure falling, the exchange rate unrealistically high, price inflation – though still high – beginning to decelerate, unemployment soaring, the CBI Trends Survey reporting virtually no shortages of materials, components, skilled labour or plant capacity.

That is a strange period to look back on. There appeared to be a great gulf between attitudes in much of the City and in industry throughout the country. In some quarters there was a Khomeini-like fanaticism abroad, a reluctance to see the connection between high interest rates and a crippling exchange rate. North Sea oil had made sterling a petro-currency, it was alleged; the days of manufacturing industry were over.

'And there were good reasons,' writes Alan Walters,

> for believing that part of the appreciation [of sterling] was due to the increase in the price of oil in 1979. The real question was how much could be attributed to oil prices? So far as I know, there was no rigorous effort to examine critically the proposition that the oil-price increase accounted for virtually all the appreciation.

Niehans conjectured that only some 20 per cent of the appreciation could be attributed to the rise in the price of oil – and I still find no good reason to disagree with that figure. It was clear that the monetary squeeze was the dominant cause of the appreciation. (1986)

Walters concluded that monetary policy was too tight and that the authorities had been misled through concentrating on M3. 'Over the years,' he writes, 'the UK approximation to transactions money has been M1, that is currency plus sight deposits at the banks. ... Yet ... the definition that was adopted in the MTFS was for sterling M3 – about 60 per cent of which is interest-bearing credit instruments which are not used for transactions purposes.'

He goes on: 'The attempt by the authorities to contain the burgeoning £M3 statistics took the form of raising short-term interest rates through the Minimum Lending Rate (MLR) mechanism in an effort to sell more government debt to offset the additional bank lending. But as an inadvertent outcome, the MLR increase induced a severe squeeze on *transactions* money M1 and the monetary base.'

'Thus,' he comments, 'the MTFS and political reputations were based on the volatile credit base of £M3.' However, political reputations appear to have survived. Parts of British industry did not.

In the second half of 1980 MLR was lowered from 16 per cent, at which it then stood, to 14 per cent, and at the time of the 1981 budget it was lowered again to 12 per cent, which appeared to have a reviving effect on narrow money. The government was not yet ready to abandon M3 as the centrepiece of the financial strategy, but the targets were raised, and the implied intention was to respond less slavishly to the M3 statistics in making interest rate changes. In the words of the 1981 Red Book, 'the significance of short run movements for interest rate policy will be interpreted in the light of other financial developments.' The demotion of M3 in subsequent annual Red Books, first to sharing pride of place with narrow money, and then disappearing altogether in favour of MO, is illustrated in the little chart in table 2.

Table 2   The Medium Term Financial Strategy

Date of Financial Statement and Budget Report	Description of targets set in the MTFS
March 1980	Target range for £M3.
March 1981	Ditto.
March 1982	Single target range which applies to both broad and narrow measures of money: £M3 (and PSL2) and M1.
March 1983	Ditto.
March 1984	Separate target ranges for narrow money (MO) and for £M3.
March ˜	Separate target ranges for narrow money (MO) and £M3. Projections of money GDP shown as assumptions on which the monetary target ranges are based.
March 1986	Projections of money GDP as the Government's objectives. Target ranges for MO and £M3.
March 1987	Projections of money GDP as the Government's objectives. Target range for MO.
March 1988	Ditto.

However, to revert for the time being to the 1981 Budget, while supporting a relaxation of monetary policy, Walters was arguing for a tightening of fiscal policy, that is, for a reduced borrowing requirement. In this, according to William Keegan, (*Mrs Thatcher's Economic Experiment*, 1986) he was allied with John Hoskyns, the Head of the Policy Unit, and also David Wolfson, another adviser in the Policy Unit.

The Treasury, which had of its own accord planned on the assumption that the medium term strategy would require a lower borrowing requirement, came under pressure for one lower still. The Walters/Hoskyns axis won the day with the Prime Minister and, in due course, with the Chancellor. In the depths of a slump, when practically everyone was expecting the

Budget to bring some relief to the economy, it set out to reduce the PSBR from the £13.5 billion then estimated for 1980–1 to £10.5 billion in 1981–2; that is, from 6 per cent to 4.5 per cent of GDP. Since public expenditure was rising, this aim could be achieved, as Nick Gardner puts it in *Decade of Discontent* (1987), only by 'the largest increase in taxation ever introduced in a single year, taking British taxation as a proportion of GDP to a record level. He had done so, moreover, at a time when the economy was in the deepest recession experienced by any industrial country since the war. ... Above all, a demand reduction on that scale, and at that time, constituted a more extreme departure from the former Keynesian consensus than had anywhere been attempted.'

Though others – including the dissidents in the Cabinet, various of whom were dropped or demoted later in the year – were aghast at these developments, the 1981 Budget passed into the folklore of the New Right as a great victory. Moreover, it set a pattern for the Budgets to come. Whatever the setbacks on the public expenditure front, whatever variations in the money supply targets, both in the choice of aggregate to be targeted and in the numbers attached to the targets, a progressive reduction in the PSBR in relation to national income became a consistent feature of fiscal policy, year after year, even when this meant raising taxes or at least forgoing tax cuts. This was in sharp contrast to the conduct of affairs on the other side of the Atlantic by the Reagan administration which, having promised a balanced budget, financed tax cuts and massive defence spending by means of an enormous budget deficit.

In the months following the 1981 Budget, the British economy touched the bottom of the slump. Up to a point this reflected what was happening in the rest of the industrialised world. No economy is an island; the closed economy exists, as a deliberate abstraction, only in text books. The quadrupling of prices by the oil producers in 1979 sucked purchasing power out of the oil-using economies, and growth had slowed down in all the main industrialised countries. But in Britain, growth actually went into reverse; in 1981 Britain was the only major economy where output was less than in 1979.

From this low point, things started to get better from the second half of 1981 – everything except unemployment, which continued to increase. Output turned up and developed what emerged as a growth rate of 2 per cent, in spite of a dip in the world economy in 1982. There was a rise in productivity in manufacturing industry. But the most remarkable turn for the better came on the inflation front, where the rate of price increases came down into single figures during 1982 and dipped below 5 per cent in the spring of 1983, after which it fluctuated around 5 per cent.

From a monetarist point of view it was natural to regard this as a victory for policies designed to reduce the growth of the money supply as the essential means of reducing inflation. A non-monetarist view was that the slowing down of inflation was due, on the external side, to falling commodity prices – including a fall in the price of oil from its 1979 peak – and, domestically, to the damping down of wages pressures through closures and unemployment; and that these in turn could be accounted for by the recession sparked off by the 1979 oil crisis and exacerbated by fiscal policy, high interest rates and an uncompetitive exchange rate. The fact remained that inflation was down, without reliance on a statutory pay and prices policy such as Edward Heath's, which had broken down, or on co-operation from the trade unions, which had finally been withdrawn from James Callaghan.

There were monetarists who, in spite of this result, were disappointed that the government had not adopted their particular prescription for controlling the monetary base, that is, the reserves held by the banks with the Bank of England plus notes and coin, also known as MO; this option appeared at one time, in the government's early days, to be receiving serious consideration, but it was not adopted. Later, in the 1987 and 1988 versions of the MTFS, MO was to be the sole monetary aggregate to be targeted, but that was never described as control of the monetary base.

The semantic problem of the use of the terms *control* and *target*, and the question of whether it was ever believed, as this use of language suggests, that the authorities could literally control the targeted aggregates, has been discussed earlier in this chapter. However that may be, by 1982 the targeted aggregates were increasingly seen and described as *indicators* of monetary conditions and a guide to the need for a change in interest rates, to be taken into account along with other indicators.

In both the 1982 and 1983 versions of the MTFS, the target (revised upwards in 1982) was set in terms of a single growth path for 'both narrow and broad measures of money: M1 and £M3 (and PSL2)', which embraces building society deposits; but, in the words of the 1983 Red Book, '... the interpretation of monetary conditions will continue to take account of all the available evidence, including the exchange rate, structural changes in financial markets, saving behaviour, and the level and structure of interest rates.'

The new emphasis on the exchange rate was significant. In 1981 recognition that the pound was overvalued had led to attempts to manipulate interest rates and, in consequence, the exchange rate on a downward course, but a brake was applied to interest rate reductions by downward movements in the pound in the autumn of 1981 and the period November 1982 to March 1983; these were felt to have gone too far and to threaten a resurgence in inflationary expectations – though there was another school of thought that a further depreciation in the pound was required to restore industrial competitiveness. This was part of the background from which the pursuit of exchange rate stability was to emerge, though the time was not yet ripe for it to be avowed as an overt policy objective.

In spite of the fluctuations in the exchange rate and interest rates, the latter were about 6.5 per cent below their October 1981 level by the time of the 1983 budget and the run-up to the 1983 general election. Monetary growth appeared to have been within the revised target range of 8–12 per cent for both wide and narrow money during the past year; a fresh target range of 7–11 per cent was set for the coming year. The PSBR as a percentage of GDP had been reduced in each of the last two years, and was projected to remain unchanged in the coming year, though in the event it was fractionally higher. In this, his fifth and final budget, Geoffrey Howe was able to announce some tax reliefs; but, since expenditure, though now under better control, was higher than when the government took office, so too was taxation (including national insurance contributions). Output growth seemed set fair to continue though, since measurements of GDP are uncertain at the time and subject to later revision, the strength of the recovery was not yet clear. The great victory, apart from the Falklands, was on the inflation front; the great setback was the rise in unemployment, which still continued, though at a lower rate of increase in 1980 and 1981.

13

Monetary Policy and the MTFS – the Second Term

The course of the economy ran altogether smoother, in most respects, in the Conservative government's second four-year term. Recovery was sustained throughout the period. The rate of growth rose to over 3 per cent a year; the miners' strike in 1984–85 was followed by a brief flattening of the upward trend, but growth was then resumed. Unemployment, the dark side of the generally bright picture, continued to rise for most of the second term but flattened out for a few months in 1985, then rose again but fell consistently from mid-1986 onwards. The exchange rate and interest rates had their ups and downs, the pound falling to near parity with the dollar early in 1985 but then rising again.

The inflation rate fluctuated around 5 per cent in the period 1983 to 1985, but fell to 3 per cent in April 1986, the lowest for 18 years. It did not continue its downward progress towards the government's objective of stable prices, or zero inflation, but fluctuated below 5 per cent – a major achievement but still a high enough rate to halve the value of money in less than 20 years.

What of the MTFS? Having already served a four-year stint by 1984, which qualifies as a reasonable medium-term period, it could in theory have been pensioned off. In practice that course was probably never a genuine option from the point of view of market psychology. For that matter, when – from that point of view – will this government ever have the option of laying the MTFS to rest?

So the period of the MTFS, in the words of the Red Book, was extended in 1984, but separate target ranges were adopted for broad and narrow money, £M3 and MO respectively. This twinning of targets was continued in the next two years, but increasingly £M3 was given houseroom on sufferance only; like other measures of broad money, it had ceased to be a reliable indicator of monetary conditions and of the need for a change in interest rates. As the 1985 Red Book put it:

'Over the past five years, households have increased both their borrowing and their holdings of liquid financial assets. This build-up of wider liquidity seems to have reflected an increase in the demand for liquid assets as a form of savings. It has been consistent with lower inflation and a steady decline in the growth of money GDP. As a result, the significance of the broad aggregates as monetary indicators has somewhat diminished.

The argument is taken to its logical conclusion in the Treasury article on 'Broad Money and Inflation', to which I have already referred in the previous chapter. 'Liquidity has grown fast,' writes the author of the article. 'But as long as it is not spent, it cannot cause inflation.' This seems to explode the whole notion that growth in the money stock in itself is the cause of inflation. Inert deposits in banks or building societies are no more inflationary than the French peasant's fabled hoard of gold coins in a sock under the mattress.

The task of announcing that £M3 was to be dropped as a monetary target, after all the weight that had once been placed on it and all that had been done in its name, fell to the Governor of the Bank of England, Robin Leigh-Pemberton in October 1986. In the 1987 MTFS, MO – the narrowest of the measures of money in use – was the only monetary aggregate for which a target range was set; but by then the Treasury had adopted a growth path for money GDP also, a subject to which we will return shortly.

In a subsequent explanation of the dethronement of £M3 (in the course of his Mais lecture at the City University Business School in May 1987), Leigh-Pemberton spoke as follows:

The simple, easily understood rule which a £M3 target represented was no doubt always an oversimplification. Indeed this was acknowledged, as the policy framework evolved, through the addition of further targets and the progressive elaboration of some of the many other factors necessarily 'taken into account' in the real-world process of policy decision-making.

Initially, in the high-inflation environment of the time, that oversimplification served a useful purpose, adding credibility to the authorities' counter-inflationary resolve. Subsequently, frequent redefinition of the targeted aggregate and upward revision of the target range – often missed even so – resulted in public confusion rather than confidence, and it was for this reason that we have not set a broad money target for this year.

Having explained the reasons for the change, the Governor went on to explain it away. 'In practice,' he said,

> little of substance has changed. The £M3 rule has never operated in a purely mechanical way; we have always been prepared to override its signals in the light of other, contrary, evidence. ... Equally the absence of a £M3 target emphatically does not mean that the behaviour of broad money and credit is regarded as of any less importance than before. ... The reality, with or without any particular target, is that policy is directed pragmatically. Given this reality, public confidence in policy is likely to depend on the deeds of the authorities rather than their words.

This expression of the plain man's view of monetary policy, if there can be such a thing, is an interesting passage. In arguing that nothing had really changed, it was no doubt meant to be reassuring, like Harold Wilson's assurance, at the time of the 1967 devaluation, that the pound in our pocket had not been devalued. The somewhat dismissive remarks about targets, and the elevation of pragmatism as a guiding principle, might have been taken to imply that the MTFS had become unimportant. If so, the Treasury would not have shared that view. The overdue relegation of M3 to a supporting role, though a talking point of some interest at the time, did not downgrade the significance of the MTFS itself. At the very least, to clad pragmatism in a conceptual framework, in the shape of the MTFS which symbolised the commitment to contain inflation, must have been seen by the Treasury as having a continuing importance for public confidence and for the Treasury's own sense of purpose. The Treasury would also accord it a more substantial continuing role as the framework for decisions on expenditure and taxation. It is certainly invoked, to this day, to discourage arguments for more generous expenditure policies.

Throughout the life of the MTFS, monetary policy and the containment of inflation had relied on two instruments: control of the public sector's demand for money through a low PSBR, and restraint on the private sector's demand for money by the use of interest rates. But the intellectual rationale for the use of these instruments had undergone change. By 1987 the money supply had given way, as a central concept, to money GDP – the total of money *spent* in the economy, rather than the *stock* of money in the banks – a conceptual shift for which Samuel Brittan, the most influential of the financial commentators, had been arguing for some time.

'Monetary and fiscal policies are designed to reduce the growth of money GDP, so bringing down inflation,' said the 1987 version of the MTFS. In place of a target range for £M3, a medium-term growth path for money GDP (the increase in which was projected to fall from 7.5 per cent in 1987–8 to 5.5 per cent in 1990–1) became the most prominent set of figures in the MTFS. These figures were described, not as a target, but as objectives – though, in ordinary parlance, an objective is more like a target than an indicator is.

A further run of figures projected the assumed division of money GDP growth between higher output and inflation. Monetary and fiscal policies, said the Red Book, 'are complemented by policies to encourage enterprise, efficiency and flexibility. These policies improve the division of money GDP growth between output growth and inflation, and help the creation of jobs.' For 1987–88 the projected growth of 7.5 per cent in money GDP was assumed to be divided between 3 per cent growth in output and 4.5 per cent inflation. (A year later, the out-turn for these figures in 1987–88 was put at 9.75, 4.5 and 5 per cent respectively.) If the ultimate objective of zero inflation could ever be achieved, the whole of the rise in money GDP would represent increased output.

The notion of reducing the growth of money GDP was not, of course, something new in the Treasury's consciousness. It is arguable that this was an implicit objective of the strategy from the outset. If you regard the reduction of inflation as the ultimate objective, then of course the reduction of money GDP is an intermediate objective. This does not seem to me to diminish the significance of the change to this way of expressing the intermediate objective as compared with expressing it in terms of reducing the growth of the money stock. It seems to me at the least an interesting piece of economic history that that particular phase of monetary doctrine (which some would defend as having played a useful part in the break with the past, even if the doctrine itself was imperfect) has been worked out of our system. None of this is meant to imply that we can safely ignore what is happening to the monetary aggregates.

A complication about setting one's compass by GDP, which is the measure of what the whole economy is doing, is that – quite apart from the problem of achieving the growth objective – it is not practicable even to estimate what GDP is doing on a day-to-day or a week-by-week basis, but only with a time-lag, and even then with the risk of subsequent revision of the estimates. The great virtue, therefore, which the Treasury sees in M0 as a 'target' is that it is the monetary aggregate which, over recent years, has had the most stable relationship with money GDP; it could therefore be regarded as a sort of early-warning system for the behaviour of money GDP. More concretely, 'M0 has proved a reliable indicator of monetary conditions. ... If the underlying growth of M0 threatens to move significantly outside its target range ... there is a presumption that the Government will take action on interest rates unless other indicators suggest that monetary conditions remain satisfactory.'

Of the other financial indicators, the exchange rate was singled out for particular attention. The Chancellor of the Exchequer, Nigel Lawson, had emerged as a leading advocate internationally of exchange rate stability. It was no secret that he would have liked the UK to join the exchange rate mechanism of the European Monetary System, which would have been conducive to a stable exchange rate between sterling and other European currencies – in particular the Deutschmark, a bastion of low inflation – but that the Prime Minister could not be persuaded to agree to this course. It was generally believed that, as a second best to full membership of the EMS (the UK having adhered to certain other provisions of the system but not to participation in the crucial exchange rate mechanism), it was Treasury policy to 'shadow' the Deutschmark and, through the use of interest rates and intervention in the foreign exchange market, to keep the DM–sterling exchange rate within a range of DM 2.80–3.00 to the pound, as a pressure on British manufacturers to keep cost increases down to the same rate as their German competitors. The posture of the authorities was that higher inflation would not be accommodated by domestic monetary expansion or by external depreciation, and a fall in the exchange rate would be a signal of inflationary pressures in the economy and of the need to raise interest rates.

The virtual adoption of an exchange rate target had a more tangible effect than the adoption of money GDP as a medium-term objective. However, apart from getting us off the £M3 hook, the new presentation of the MTFS probably had more intellectual validity for a good many people; it might also be read as compatible with a greater emphasis on economic growth in the claims made for the government's achievements, not at the expense of the price stability objective but as an objective which could be pursued concurrently. The language of the MTFS continued to reiterate that 'Economic policy is set in a nominal framework', and the Treasury remained as sensitive as ever to any suggestion of a change in policy. But the fact is that GDP is a measure not only of expenditure (and income) but also of output. The objective for money GDP can therefore be viewed as, in effect, an objective for growth in real GDP with low inflation – the El Dorado of economic policy over the decades. The difference is that, if it should come again to a tug of war between the two, the MTFS would require priority to be given to the anti-inflation objective.

Under Geoffrey Howe and Nigel Lawson the Treasury did not seek the lead in industrial policy which, because of Denis

Healey's interests and force of character, it had exercised in his day. Under the Conservative government, the Treasury retained its liaison function with the National Economic Development Office, and the Chancellor chaired meetings of the National Economic Development Council, but those bodies were not held in the same esteem as before and came close to being abolished. After something of a cliffhanger, they survived, but the frequency of Council meetings was reduced.

The lead in 'supply side' measures passed largely to the Department of Trade and Industry and the Department of Employment. (The latter Department, especially when David Young was its Secretary of State and had the Prime Minister's ear, succeeded in getting an amount of Exchequer money for employment and training measures which was a cause of great chagrin to the expenditure side of the Treasury.) Nevertheless, the Treasury would have claimed that the Chancellor's policies were directed towards improving the performance of the economy. Equally, growth of output and therefore of revenue, with a little help from the proceeds of privatisation, was the route to reversing the rise in the burden of taxation and national insurance.

A declared feature of Nigel Lawson's approach to taxation was to eliminate special concessions (such as the tax relief for insurance policies) but to reduce rates of tax. Thus, the rates of corporation tax had been reduced while special capital allowances for companies had been cut out. But in his first two budgets the Chancellor, while raising tax thresholds, did not have sufficient room for manoeuvre to reduce the rates of personal taxation. The basic rate of income tax had stood at 30 per cent since June 1979, when the new government had cut it from 33 per cent, while abolishing the reduced rate band of 25 per cent which had existed before then. At last, in the 1986 Budget, the basic rate was cut to 29p – a modest beginning, with the prospect of further cuts to come.

In 1987 – once again in the run-up to a general election – the Chancellor was able to open his Budget speech by declaring that 'We are now entering our seventh successive year of steady growth, and the fifth in which this has been combined with low inflation,' and to bring it to a climax by announcing a reduction in the basic rate of income tax by 2p to 27 per cent. At the same time, the PSBR was still coming down. For most of the government's life it had been necessary to sacrifice the objective of lower taxation to the objective of lower borrowing. Now, in the last couple of years of the second term, it was becoming possible to move towards both objectives.

14

The Budget of 1988 and After

In the weeks before the Budget of March 1988 the Treasury had to cope with an unusual dilemma. To judge by many of the indicators, including an escalation in house prices, economic growth had crossed the line into overheating of the economy and there were growing inflationary pressures; this, if one believed in interest rates as the prime instrument for short-term management of the economy, pointed to a rise in interest rates. But the demand for sterling was pushing the exchange rate above the DM 2.80–3.00 range, creating a risk of loss of competitiveness by British industry, as its prices became more expensive in other currencies while its competitors' prices became cheaper in terms of sterling. Intervention by the Bank of England (i.e. selling sterling to buy foreign currencies) by itself proved insufficient to stop the upward pressure on sterling, and a reduction in interest rates appeared to be necessary in order to reduce the attractions of holding sterling.

The indicators thus pointed in opposite directions at the same time. This was in a sense a throw-back to earlier times, when the problem of pursuing all the Treasury's objectives at the same time – growth, low inflation and a strong balance of payments – was a commonplace of economic discussion. But the conjunction of a strong pound with a weak current account was a new scenario which had not been anticipated in the MTFS.

In a sense, the strength of sterling was perverse, when the current account of the balance of payments was moving into substantial deficit. At that stage the Treasury forecast of the deficit for 1988–89 was £4 billion, which it would be possible to finance without difficulty, but estimates of the deficit were unreliable because of problems with the balance of payments statistics.

The events of that month are very recent history and need be only briefly retold. Attitudes had moved a long way from those of 1980–81. Some who had then accepted the need for a shock to the prevailing psychology in industry, in spite of the damage to output and employment, had no wish to see a repetition of that experience. Financial commentators generally appeared to recognise the dilemma. There was no talk this time of sterling being a petro-currency or of writing off manufacturing industry.

But there were some, including the Bank of England, who thought that, in the face of this dilemma, inflation remained enemy number one and fighting it must have over-riding priority. Brian Griffiths, a committed monetarist and free-market man who was now head of the No. 10 Policy Unit, and Alan Walters, now back in Washington but still functioning as a sort of offshore adviser who made occasional descents on Whitehall, were believed to take this view. According to apparently well informed press reports, at a meeting on 4 March 1988 with the Chancellor and the Governor, the Prime Minister sided with Leigh-Pemberton and over-ruled Lawson. Large-scale intervention was to cease and interest rates were not to be lowered. On the following Monday there was no intervention and no reduction in interest rates, and the exchange rate rose above the DM 3.00 mark.

One of the concerns of the monetarist school, according to the press, was that the foreign currencies acquired through intervention added to the money supply and had an inflationary effect. The foreign currencies themselves could have no such effect, since they were salted away in the Exchange Equalisation Account, but the sterling to pay for them was raised in the first instance by short-term borrowing for the EEA, which could affect the money supply. However, Treasury policy was to fund these borrowings in the course of the year by sales of government securities outside the banking system. Given that the rest of government borrowing was very low – negative, in fact, as we shall see – it is unlikely that this particular argument loomed large in the differences of view between No. 10 and No. 11.

The remarkable thing about this disagreement was not that it occurred but that it was so well reported and so publicly aired through conflicting statements by the two ministers in the Commons and through press briefings. It was believed that Nigel Lawson was not so much concerned about defending his upper limit of DM 3.00, a line which would in any event have been hard to hold at that stage, but about the damage to his policy of a managed float of sterling rather than a free float, and to his standing as the minister responsible for economic policy. When a reduction in interest rates did take place, after the Budget, it was widely regarded as a symbol of his right to manage. (Three reductions of 0.5 per cent each were, however, followed by three increases in the space of three months.)

There may be precedents for open differences of view between a Prime Minister and a serving member of Cabinet – the case of Tony Benn and Harold Wilson comes to mind – but not between a Prime Minister and the Chancellor of the Exchequer. When Peter Thorneycroft failed to get Harold Macmillan's support for cuts in Estimates in 1958, he resigned. A Chancellor of the Exchequer cannot be effective without the backing of the Prime Minister. Clearly public dissension between Margaret Thatcher and Nigel Lawson could not go on, and it was in fact brought to an end by an agreed statement, reconciling their points of view, delivered by the Prime Minister. Having been blown off course by these events, the Treasury's hopes of getting its strategy back on course now depended on less perverse reactions by the foreign exchange market to a deteriorating current account of the balance of payments.

These dramatic events would have overshadowed any run-of-the-mill Budget, but the Budget of 15 March 1988 was itself a piece of high drama. It had been expected that the Chancellor would have room both to reduce the PSBR and to cut tax rates as a result of continued growth in output, which the Chancellor put in his Budget speech at close to 4.5 per cent for 1987 as a whole and which, in the fourth quarter of 1987, was 5 per cent higher than in the fourth quarter a year earlier. The reductions in the PSBR and in tax rates announced in the Budget speech exceeded expectations.

Two measures stand out. First, the basic rate of income tax was reduced to 25p, on top of a more generous increase in thresholds than the indexation of allowances normally required by statute. (This requirement, which could be over-ridden by a resolution of the House, stemmed from the 'Rooker-Wise' amendment initiated by two back-benchers in the time of the last Labour government.) A further reduction of the basic rate to 20p was held out as an objective for the future.

Second, a single higher rate of 40p was substituted for the previous five higher rates ranging from 40p to 60p. The Conservative government had inherited a top rate of no less than 83p on earned income, which they immediately reduced to 60p, while increasing Value Added Tax to 15 per cent. (There had also been a surcharge of 15p on investment income – producing a top rate of 98p – which was abolished in 1984.) This further reduction of the top rate from 60p to 40p, at a stroke, was the most dramatic and the most controversial feature of the Budget.

In addition, the indexation of capital gains, which had been introduced in 1982 and extended in 1985, was now taken further, by re-basing capital gains to 1982. That is to say, no tax would be charged on any capital gains which arose before that date, and which might therefore represent purely paper gains arising from inflation. The rates of tax on capital gains arising after 1982 were aligned with the new income tax rates of 25p and 40p. The rate of inheritance tax was also reduced to 40p and the threshold for this tax was raised. Thus there was a simplification of the rates for all these taxes. A further major change was a plan to move in 1990 to independent taxation for husbands and wives; minor changes included a further reduction of special tax reliefs, in line with the objective of lower tax rates combined with fewer special reliefs.

A further highlight of the Budget speech, following an almost routine reiteration of the Medium Term Financial Strategy, was the announcement that in 1987–88, the year then ending, the Public Sector Borrowing requirement would be less than zero; there would be a public sector debt repayment. (The last

Chancellor to achieve this, whom Nigel Lawson refrained from mentioning by name, had been Roy Jenkins in Harold Wilson's first Labour administration.) This result had been made possible by buoyant tax revenue and by 'lower than expected public expenditure' (much of it due in fact to higher receipts rather than lower spending). Having achieved a balanced Budget, the Chancellor declared that he intended to stick to it: 'In other words, henceforth a zero PSBR will be the norm.' There were bound to be fluctuations on either side from year to year; for 1988–89 he had decided to budget for a further public sector debt repayment of some £3 billion.

The Budget of 1988 was a great coup for Nigel Lawson. It was the culmination of tax policies pursued in a series of Budgets since he had become Chancellor, and of a fiscal strategy in which he had played a part even before that as Financial Secretary to the Treasury.

It was of course an inegalitarian Budget; many were bound to contrast the large tax reliefs to the already wealthy with the reshuffling of social security benefits among the poor which was debated in the Commons only a few days later. But the Budget decisions, as we have already noted, are in practice about taxes, not about expenditure, which is settled beforehand, leaving the field clear for the tax decisions.

The charge of ineglitarianism could be brought not just against this particular Budget but against the whole series of tax changes since 1979. Anyone on average male earnings of £244.70 a week in 1988–89 would, according to Treasury figures, be paying a fractionally higher percentage of his gross income in direct and indirect taxes, national insurance contributions and local rates than ten years previously; for a married person, and more so for one with two children, the increase would be more visible – from 38.5 per cent to 40.5 per cent. The figures showed a similar increase in the percentage of gross income paid as tax, etc. by anyone on half or three quarters of average earnings.

On the other hand, those with twice average earnings would be paying a few percentage points less in tax, etc. than in 1978–79. Those earning five times the average – £1,233.50 a week – an amount earned by only a small minority but not uncommon among senior executives and such like – would be paying much less in tax, etc. – about 15 per cent less of their gross income – than in 1978–79, and so on.

The Chancellor did not make any claim to being an egalitarian. The list of his tax objectives (in a pamphlet on 'Tax Reform: the Government's Record', which was published in June 1988) did not include redistribution of income but, on the contrary, 'to leave people more of their own money, so that they can choose for themselves what to do with it'. His main stated objective in reforming taxes had been to improve the performance of the economy,

In present-day Conservative philosophy, it is not a bad thing if inequality is growing, provided that everyone is better off; and this, it is claimed, is what has been happening – at least in respect of those at work – because of the improved performance of the economy. According to a further set of Treasury estimates, real take-home pay in 1988–89 will show an increase at every level of earnings, ranging from an increase of around 25 per cent (for anyone on half average male earnings) to well over 60 per cent (for a person on five times average male earnings) as compared with ten years earlier. These figures are for single people, but the percentage increases in take-home pay for married people, with or without children, do not differ greatly.

Most of this improvement in real take-home pay had taken place in the period after 1982–83, after recovery from the slump of 1980 and 1981 had begun; the increase in real earnings had been made possible by six years of uninterrupted growth averaging a little over 3 per cent a year, with a further year of growth in prospect. This was much the same as the average growth experienced in the 1950s and 1960s, until the quadrupling of oil prices in 1973 brought to a close that golden era of growth in the industrialised countries, and the further escalation of oil prices in 1979 was followed by recession; but it could be claimed that, whereas Britain had then lagged behind other countries in its growth rate, it now led. It was also claimed that growth was now steadier, and that this was due to the foreswearing of Keynesian practices of short-term demand management; no credit was given to the benefit of North Sea oil to the balance of payments and its part in relieving the economy of the periodical sterling crises of earlier decades and the resulting stop–go cycle.

It was the growth in national output and income which had led to the improvement (in absolute terms) in net after-tax incomes, even though, in proportionate terms, the burden of taxation (including national insurance contributions and local authority rates) was still higher as a percentage of GDP after the 1988 Budget than it had been in 1970–71 – just under 38 per cent as compared with just over 36 per cent. This comes as something of a surprise after the dramatic cuts in rates of personal tax, but these had in part been paid for by increased VAT payments; by the ending of special tax reliefs for new life assurance policies, for foreign earnings, for non-charitable covenants, and for new home improvement loans; and by more than doubling the taxation of company cars, a perk exceptionally widespread in Britain. The reductions in rates of corporation tax had been made possible by phasing out the special relief for capital expenditure (a 100 per cent first year allowance which had been introduced for manufacturing industry generally at the time of Edward Heath's U-turn) and stock relief (introduced in Denis Healey's time). The Chancellor's aim had been to charge lower rates of tax on a broader tax base; this policy, he believed, removed distortions and improved incentives.

As a tailpiece to this summary account of taxation since 1979, it is interesting that Nigel Lawson's pamphlet contains not a single word about the plan to switch from local authority domestic rates to the so-called community charge, more accurately known as a poll tax, a further ineaglitarian measure. It is true that the Secretary of State for the Environment, as the minister responsible for local authority affairs, and not the Chancellor, was in the lead on this, but the title of the pamphlet did refer to 'the *Government's* Record'. The Treasury (including myself) had always seen more merit than probably most people did in the rates as a local property tax, easily understood and administered, and clearly related to a visible local asset; and the Chancellor was believed to be unenthusiastic about the poll tax, but not to the point of prolonged opposition, since it was after all not his baby.

As for the PSBR, the Chancellor was able to claim that '...
even if there had been no privatisation proceeds at all, the
resulting PSBR, at 0.5 per cent of GDP, would still have been the
lowest in all but one year since the beginning of the 1950s.'
Privatisation proceeds had nevertheless expedited the programme of cuts in tax rates which had paved the way for the
1988 Budget. And if we are to indulge in what-might-have
beens, we should not leave taxes and royalties from North Sea oil
out of account. The Labour government got practically no
benefit from North Sea oil. We can only speculate what
difference it would have made to the history of our times if this
new revenue had come on stream a few years earlier.

From a little over £0.5 billion in 1978–79, revenues from the
North Sea had risen to £12 billion in 1984–85, after which they
began to decline along with the collapse in oil prices. As can be
seen from table 3, in 1984–85, other things being equal, the PSBR
would have been no less than £24.2 billion. But other things
would not have been unchanged, and the whole course of events,
including the state of the balance of payments, would have been
different.

This is not to suggest that North Sea revenues are in the same
category as privatisation proceeds – though they are a new item
and one which is generally believed to have a limited life ahead
of it – or that the Treasury should publish notional figures of the
PSBR excluding North Sea revenues. The point is simply that
the Chancellor has in this respect been lucky. But then the
Romans used to regard being lucky as one of the attributes of a
successful leader.

Both privatisation proceeds and North Sea revenues were
more important in reducing the PSBR in the years leading up to
1987–88 than in the 1988 Budget itself. Even without them, the
PSBR in that Budget – other things being equal, which, again,
they would not have been – would have been low by the
standards of earlier years, though a balanced Budget would have
been unlikely.

But why should a balanced Budget – a zero PSBR – be the
norm, rather than low government borrowing financed outside
the banking system, which would be generally regarded as non-

Table 3   Public Sector Borrowing

	PSBR: Cash (£ billion)	PSBR: ratio to GDP (per cent)	PSBR excluding privatisation proceeds (£ billion)	Revenue from oil and gas* (£ billion)	PSBR excluding privatisation proceeds and revenue from oil and gas (£ billion)
1978–79	9·2	5·25	9·2	0·6	9·8
1979–80	9·9	4·75	10·3	2·3	12·6
1980–81	12·5	5·25	12·9	3·7	16·6
1981–82	8·6	3·25	9·1	6·5	15·6
1982–83	8·9	3·25	9·4	7·8	17·2
1983–84	9·7	3·25	10·8	8·8	19·6
1984–85	10·1	3·00	12·2	12·0	24·2
1985–86	5·7	1·50	8·4	11·3	19·7
1986–87	3·4	1·00	7·9	4·8	12·7
1987–88 (estimated out-turn)	−3·5	−0·75	1·6	4·7	6·3
1988–89 (Budget forecast)	−3·2	−0·75	1·8		

*Taxes and Royalties Attributable to UK and UKCS Oil and Gas (excluding gas levy)
Compiled from various Treasury figures.

inflationary and would create no significant interest rate problem? Why not a PSBR equal to, say, 1 per cent of GDP? The answers are not altogether explicit. One concrete reason given in the Budget speech is that the lower the amount of government borrowing, the smaller the amount of debt interest in public expenditure, which has to be financed out of taxation or by further borrowing. More important, probably, a balanced Budget is a simpler concept, designed to have the maximum confidence effect. Given that there were bound to be fluctuations round any norm that was chosen, better to fluctuate round a zero PSBR than any higher figure. Although a future government would not be bound by the norm of a balanced Budget, in psychological terms they would be that much more constrained from moving too far away from it. (Perhaps a similar thought had played a part in cutting the top rate of tax to as low a figure as 40 per cent; a later Chancellor might increase it, but would probably feel some constraint against raising it to a very high figure.) If this effect were achieved, the 1988 Budget would have succeeded in changing the rules of the game.

In the months following the Budget, as signs of inflation persisted and the balance of payments deficit on current account was clearly going to be much larger than had been forecast at the time of the Budget – perhaps three times as large – there were criticisms in the press both that the short-lived lowering of interest rates had been ill judged and that the Budget had been too expansionary and had put too much money into people's pockets. The implication, not always made explicit, was that the Budget surplus and the reduction in the national debt, which at first impact had been generally received as a triumphant climax to years of prudent budgeting, ought to have been even larger.

Nigel Lawson, in a phrase rivalling Denis Healey's remark about tiny Chinese minds, dismissed his critics as teenage scribblers. But in fact the Treasury were bound to be concerned about a reduced propensity to save and an insatiable propensity to spend and consume in the personal sector and must have been considering how to tighten monetary policy. The three increases in interest rates to restore them to their pre-Budget level were followed by a series of further half-point increases; this could be done without jacking up the exchange rate too violently, though it was still well outside the previous 'target' of a DM 3.00 limit. There was a general expectation of further increases to come, and it was a matter for speculation whether the upsurge in bank lending and consumer spending could be contained purely by the interest rate instrument. To put these concerns into perspective, inflation was now considered to be going in the wrong direction when it rose above 4 per cent, and was not to be judged by the runaway rates of inflation of an earlier phase. Nevertheless, when the Chancellor spoke of the prospect of a rise to 6 per cent inflation before it came down again, there was bound to be trouble on the public expenditure front, since the programme limits did not allow for such a rise in costs.

Gossip about the state of relations between No. 10 and No. 11, and about the occupancy of the latter in the somewhat longer term, was refuelled during July when it was made known that

Alan Walters was to return the following year as an in-house rather than an offshore adviser at No. 10. Walters, a highly individualistic person, made this the occasion to give interviews in which he voiced his criticisms of Lawson's exchange rate policy in general and the temporary reductions in interest rates in particular. This would have been unacceptable conduct on the part of an official adviser, and was at the least an indiscretion on the part of an adviser designate. Samuel Brittan, who had adopted the role of champion of Nigel Lawson and critic of the Prime Minister ever since the difference between the two had surfaced, was now moved to launch an acrimonious attack, in the *Financial Times* and on television, against the undermining of the Chancellor's position and against Walters' behaviour, and to pour scorn on the idea of of a Cecil Parkinson/Alan Walters axis in Nos 10 and 11, which some were prognosticating. However, it was indicated that No. 10 did not want a recurrence of public dissension when it was made known that Walters had been asked to make no more public statements. This came too late, and the damage had been done, according to Brittan, who appeared to believe that the Prime Minister had at least implicitly sanctioned Walters' remarks, though I should be surprised if that were the case.

On the contrary, the Prime Minister went out of her way to find occasions to pay public compliments to Lawson's handling of the economy. She dispelled speculation about an Autumn ministerial reshuffle, in which Lawson might leave the Treasury, by announcing on 25 July a reshuffle which did not involve any of the three key posts – Treasury, Foreign and Commonwealth Office and Home Office – but in which the DHSS was split into two separate Departments of Health and Social Security and a number of senior and junior ministers were reposted in consequence. This split was long overdue and the announcement could have been explained on grounds which had nothing to do with Lawson; but no one doubted the significance of the timing of the announcement, as being designed to make known not only that this July reshuffle was to take place but also that there was to be no Autumn reshuffle.

There was more bad news for the Treasury in August, when

the balance of payments figures for July were published and showed a record current account deficit of £2.15 billion for that month. This brought the cumulative deficit for the year to almost £8 billion in seven months, as compared with the estimate of £4 billion for the whole year which had been made at Budget time. The Treasury had known even then that this estimate was unreliable, but it had not anticipated that the error would turn out to be as enormous as this. Immediately, on 25 August, base rates were raised by a full point to 12 per cent, and had now been raised eight times since the low point of 7½ per cent in June.

'We are returning to the good old 1960s crises,' said one City economist, quoted in *The Times* on 27 August. At the beginning of 1988, when I was in the early stages of work on this book, a former very senior colleague said to me that the situation reminded him of 1964, which we had both lived through. That was the year when the dash for growth under Reginald Maudling's Chancellorship led to a massive current account deficit and, following the Conservative government's election defeat, a number of drastic remedial measures by the incoming Labour government, including an import surcharge. The Treasury would not, of course, have accepted, at that stage in 1988, the comparison with 1964, but Brian Reading had some interesting comments on the similarities (as well as the differences) in a *Sunday Times* article on 28 August 1988, pointing out that the trade deficit in July 1988 was even higher as a percentage of GDP than the then record figure for February 1964. He compared the statement made at that time by the Prime Minister, Sir Alec Douglas-Home, that 'The economy has seldom been stronger' with Nigel Lawson's assertion that the economy was doing 'exceptionally well'.

Some of the features of earlier balance of payments crises– a drain on the gold and foreign exchange reserves or a drastic fall in the exchange rate or both – were not yet present, though there was some downward pressure on the pound and some intervention by the Bank towards the end of August to support the rate. (This was in contrast to the attempts made in June to prevent the exchange rate from rising and indicated that concern had shifted from loss of competitiveness to anxiety about inflation and the state of confidence in the currency.) As compared, for instance, with the crisis of 1976, when there was the prospect of difficulty in finding foreign exchange to finance the nation's imports, until we negotiated IMF support and the central bank credits which followed it, in the summer of 1988 we had record gold and foreign exchange reserves. These were still early days in the crisis, if there was one.

There was now widespread press criticism of the March 1988 Budget. There was adverse comment on the fact that, for many, the benefit of the tax reliefs given in March had been eroded by the higher interest charges on their mortgages. Michael Heseltine, a former member of Mrs Thatcher's cabinet, was among those to suggest the introduction of credit controls. Others suggested that fiscal action should be taken even before the next regular Budget – in the autumn perhaps – to redress the laxity of the Budget of March 1988. But if my former colleague was right, as subsequent events appeared to show, the problems lying ahead were foreseeable even before that Budget. These events suggested to me that monetary policies had not resolved the historic dilemmas involved in seeking to achieve all Britain's economic objectives – growth and high employment, low inflation and a strong balance of payments – though the difficulty had been compounded by an ambitious objective for tax reductions. Unlike previous plans for growth without inflation, which depended on human factors outside government control, the MTFS had set out to control only the inanimate monetary aggregates, but these too turned out to depend on the behaviour of people who borrowed, lent, saved and spent money.

In an article on 27 August 1988 the Economic Correspondent of *The Times* wrote as follows:

> When the Chancellor two months ago criticised the "teenage scribblers" in the City who, he said, jumped up and down to be noticed, he meant it as a joke. But it is a joke which has badly misfired. The scribblers' revenge is now coming through loud and clear, and not many City economists can avoid a smirk at Mr Lawson's expense.

The Treasury believed that interest rates were capable of

doing all or most of the job of putting things right. In the issue of *The Times* already cited, the Chancellor was reported as rejecting credit controls; interest rates would take time, he said, to have their effect, but 'In time the situation will correct itself in a satisfactory way.' Who would have the last laugh?

It is a penalty of chronicling contemporary events that the record of events, by the time it appears in print, can never be complete. This account is obliged to break off at a point when future developments, in terms both of policy and personalities, were a matter of intense interest for observers of the Treasury scene.

15

The Treasury and its Officials

The Treasury is a small, high-quality Department. At the time I left it, in the 1970s, it was smaller still, with about 1,000 staff of all grades, including secretaries, messengers and so on, of whom about 400 were on the public expenditure side, for which I was responsible. By 1988, after reabsorbing work from the now defunct Civil Service Department, and later from the equally defunct Manpower and Personnel Office, the core functions of the Treasury employed something over 1,400 people. But on top of that the Treasury had become responsible for a number of organisations which provide common services to the civil service as a whole, and which accounted for over 1,700 more staff, bringing the total into the range of 3,100–3,200.

This is still a small number compared to the giant Departments such as Inland Revenue or the Ministry of Defence. Moreover, the common service activities for the most part do not impinge on the work of the core policy divisions of the Treasury, which make up a compact Department, well knit together.

There are great advantages in this. It is good for co-ordination. The Permanent Secretary to the Treasury can gather together round his table, at short notice, the most senior officials concerned with every aspect of financial and economic policy and the control of the civil service. The Second Permanent Secretary responsible for public expenditure, in response to the latest problem on that front, can gather round *his* table the Deputy Secretaries and Under Secretaries (Grades 2 and 3 in the new nomenclature) who deal with every spending programme.

And so on. Workloads are correspondingly heavy and most Treasury officials work long hours – the more senior they are, the longer the working day.

The Permanent Secretary to the Treasury (like the Secretary of the Cabinet and the Permanent Secretary of the Civil Service Department when it was in existence) is a notch above the Permanent Secretaries of other Departments in pay and status. This gives him the authority to take the lead in economic policy matters involving a number of Departments, and to preside over a number of Second Permanent Secretaries who are in charge of different sectors of Treasury work. Officials in this grade are a notch below full Permanent Secretaries in pay but are treated equally with them in some other respects, including eligibility for a place in the honours list. When I first went to the Treasury, even the Third Secretaries, as the Treasury Deputy Secretaries were then called, all had knighthoods, but nowadays, with a few exceptions, a member of the home civil service gets his turn for a K only if he rises to Permanent Secretary or Second Permanent Secretary. In the Foreign and Commonwealth Office this distinction tends to go to others also, including many ambassadors.

The number of Second Permanent Secretaries in the Treasury has varied over the years. By 1988, after functions in the management and pay of the civil service had been restored to it, the Treasury had three Second Permanent secretaries: one in charge of the Finance sector, another in charge of Public Expenditure, and a third responsible for Civil Service Management and Pay. In addition, the Chief Economic Adviser, who is also head of the Government Economic Service, covering economists in all Departments, has the rank of Second Permanent Secretary. (The Treasury's Accounting Adviser, who is also head of the Government Accounting Service, ranks as a Deputy Secretary.)

The Finance sector embraces both what is now called Public Finance (which used to be called Home Finance) and Overseas Finance. At one time the two came under separate Second Permanent Secretaries, but they are now seen as closely inter-related – for instance, in the Medium Term Financial Strategy.

Public Finance includes fiscal and monetary policy. Overseas Finance includes our dealings with international institutions and groupings, in particular the European Community, the International Monetary Fund and the International Bank. The Second Permanent Secretary spends a great deal of his time on international meetings and consultations, and in recent years the occupant of the post has become something of a roving ambassador, while the current Permanent Secretary to the Treasury, Sir Peter Middleton, takes direct charge of the work on financial policies, which suits his personal bent.

I have mentioned the common services for which the Treasury has become responsible. The largest of these, in terms of manpower, with about 800 staff, is the Civil Service Catering Organisation (CISCO), an unlikely function for a Ministry of Finance. Next in size, with a strength of over 400, is the Central Computer and Telecommunications Agency (CCTA), which provides services in the field of information technology to the Treasury and other Departments. The Chessington Computer Centre (CCC), which also has over 400 staff, provides computerised payroll, etc. services to a number of government Departments and also to some non-Exchequer bodies. Finally, there is a small group of staff (45 in 1988) in the Rating of Government Property Department, which deals with the payment to local authorities of contributions in lieu of rates in respect of certain properties occupied by the Crown and by visiting forces.

The smallness of the Treasury can make for informality in relationships. Most Treasury officials are on first name terms with one another at all levels. They nevertheless remain conscious of the hierarchical nature of relationships in a civil service Department. Treasury ministers also commonly address their officials by their first names, but not vice versa. Relationships at this level also can be relatively informal, once ministers have settled in and have got to know their officials, but the difference in status between the political heads of Departments – who, incidentally, are very conscious of the pecking order among ministers – and the career officials is marked. While the Permanent Secretary might occasionally, though not too often, drop into the office of a colleague, ministers never set foot in the offices of their officials. (Margaret Thatcher has been an exception; in her early days as Prime Minister she embarked on a series of visits to Departments, in each of which she paid calls on a number of officials in their offices.)

Being small also makes for *esprit de corps*. The Treasury sees itself as a bastion of national solvency and the sole custodian of the taxpayer's interests. In the public expenditure field, while spending Departments view the Treasury as mean and over-powerful, the Treasury sees itself as a small beleaguered citadel of financial prudence, surrounded by spendthrift predators and surviving only by its wits and by tireless vigilance. The Treasury brings a necessary professional scepticism to bear on the expensive schemes which are constantly put to it; sometimes it may seem to the other side that this can spill over into professional unreasonableness.

The Treasury's ethos and lifestyle are austere. The top officials on the second floor have fine high-ceilinged offices, though not as grand as the Chancellor's palatial office, which was once the Air Council Chamber, then a conference room, and then converted at Anthony Barber's request because the street noise could not be kept out of his previous office. The other offices are less impressive, especially on the third floor circle, which would overlook the Treasury courtyard but for a stone balustrade which runs round the building at that level and keeps out half the light and all of the view. There are no executive dining rooms in Whitehall, but the Treasury canteen seems to have improved since my time. There are no company cars; in the Treasury the Permanent Secretary and the Second Permanent Secretaries are the only officials to have regular access to a car and driver for official purposes, but not for personal use. Wives do not accompany officials on their overseas assignments. There are no perks at all, other than the possibility, for a few, of an appearance in the honours list in the fullness of time.

A former Treasury minister who had moved to be Secretary of State in another Department once observed to me that he was conscious of a drop in the intellectual level, especially as reflected in the quality of the briefing which he received in his new Department. My own impression was that many of the senior officials there were well up to the Treasury level, but it was a bigger Department and the talent was more thinly spread. Moreover, many of its middle-level officials, who did not shine in the writing of briefs, were useful operators. Much of the Treasury's work, on the other hand, has a high policy content and is not of an operational nature, if we leave aside the recently acquired common service activities.

A good proportion of the Treasury's work consists of briefing and devilling for ministers. A great part of it consists of dealing with other Departments and with the Bank of England. Relatively little involves dealing direct with the world outside the public service, though overseas finance has always been an exception, and the work on privatisation and on financial markets and institutions has increased the amount of contact with the world at large. But none of the work involves day-to-day dealings with the general public, as does the work of, say, the Department of Social Security. A former Treasury colleague who moved to the Bank of England, where he rose rapidly, in response to a question about the differences which he found commented on the greatly increased range of contacts in his new job. One does not think of the Bank of England as a place whose officials mix all that much with the common herd, but evidently the Treasury is, or at any rate was at the time, a rather cloistered institution even by the Bank's standards.

Some Treasury staff are recruited from other Departments, on loan or for keeps, and a few from outside the public service. A good deal of effort is put into arranging for Treasury officials, in the course of their careers, to have a spell outside the Treasury, in another Department, for instance, or an overseas post, or on sabbatical leave at a univesity or business school, or in the business world or in the City – a bourne from which travellers may be tempted not to return, though generally they resist the temptation. Appearances before the Treasury and Civil Service Committee give a limited number of officials a certain amount of public exposure. Nevertheless, at official level the Treasury is not for the most part extrovert in character.

But the Chancellor, the apex of the organisation, is in the eye of the political storm. The pressures of Westminster politics are transmitted into much of the Department's work, though there are relative backwaters. The pace of events is rapid, in some areas of the work more than others, and particularly above a certain level. I can think of one or two in my time who were brought into the Treasury at or near the top, who could not catch up with the pace of the work, which therefore passed them by.

It has been alleged, for instance by William Plowden, at that time Director General of the Royal Institute of Public Administration, that there is a crisis of morale in the civil service caused by a relative deterioration in pay and conditions and a loss of esteem. The state of morale probably varies from Department to Department. For instance, the published findings of a report by the DHSS's own officials (before the split of that Department) on the administration of social security benefits recognised the low state of morale among the civil servants engaged on that work. In the Treasury, on the other hand, where things are light-years removed from life in a social security benefits office, there are factors making for high morale. The Treasury is today seen as a successful Department, which is good for morale. Departments prefer a minister who wins in Cabinet to one who cannot deliver Cabinet approval – and, in present circumstances, a Prime Ministerial blessing – for his and his Department's policies.

Nevertheless the Treasury does not appear to be immune to the malaise affecting other Departments where, it is said, a number of promising civil servants, urged to think of themselves as managers rather than policy-makers, have looked for employment as managers in the private sector for better pay. For potential rising stars in the Treasury, the financial rewards of the City are the lure. There appears to have been a significant trickle of departing talent. A boost was given a few years ago to the salaries of the top couple of tiers of the civil service – though they still do not approach top salaries in the business world – but it did not work through to the grades below. Officials engaged on privatisation, for instance, may find themselves negotiating with their opposite numbers in merchant banks earning twice as much. Only a limited number of civil servants may be presented with real options for bettering themselves in the private sector, but they are likely to be among the more able, and differentials of this size can outweigh the attractions of being at the centre of things and of working on complex matters with intellectually congenial colleagues. (There is also, it should be said, a large amount of work in the Treasury, as in most places, which is of a routine and unexciting character.)

The problem is one not merely of retaining but of recruiting talent. One gets the impression that a number of good graduates, who in earlier times might have chosen a civil service career, are now deterred by the prospect of demanding work for comparatively poor financial rewards, and opt instead for the merchant banks, which have become the honeypot for bright and ambitious young people.

It is difficult to put a finger on such an elusive thing as the intellectual level. Nor must one see the Treasury of past generations through a golden haze. Many of the top people in the Treasury when I first went there were rooted in the past, until they were succeeded by a generation of more modern outlook. Some of those under whom I served or who served under me, although intelligent enough, were ineffectual for one reason or another – unimaginative or indecisive or even neurotic. But overall the Treasury has had an edge on most other Departments, and for that matter most other organisations – though this is no guarantee of success in coping with intractable politico-economic predicaments – and it probably still has. Those whom I knew, in my time there, as promising young people are now in positions of responsibility. The areas of work of which ministers will be most conscious are still well manned. The question is whether enough promising young people are coming through behind those of my day.

A favourite topic of discussion is whether the civil service has been politicised, especially at the top levels where appointments require the Prime Minister's approval. Most knowledgeable observers do not believe that this has been so, in the normal sense of the term. In spite of the urgings of John Hoskyns, since he left the No. 10 Policy Unit, to import hundreds of 'problem solvers' from the outside world, only a limited number of political and special advisers, and of individuals with special qualifications for particular posts, have been brought in. We still have – like every other major democratic country of which I know, with the exception of the United States of America – a predominantly career service. Recruitment generally is through competitive examination; promotion to all but the two top grades is in the hands of individual Departments, employing a painstaking process of appraisal and selection. The names of candidates for promotion to the top posts are shortlisted by a small committee of Permanent Secretaries, chaired by the Secretary of the Cabinet, and submitted to the Prime Minister. Of the Permanent Secretaries appointed in Margaret Thatcher's time as Prime Minister, those whom I know would have been expected to get to the top on their abilities under any administration.

At the same time, Margaret Thatcher takes a closer interest and has more say in the general run of these appointments than did her predecessors. Her choices are likely to be candidates personally known to her, which means that it is an advantage to have served a spell in No. 10 or the Cabinet Office, but she does also come across other officials from the Treasury and other Departments. The private political affiliations or sympathies, if any, of candidates for appointments are not known or enquired about. They are not asked if they agree with the government's policies but are expected to deliver them.

In the Treasury a handful of advisers have been brought in who are committed to the Conservative cause, and a couple of specialist advisers for their professional qualifications. Ministers and their special advisers set the political tone for the Treasury's stance, perhaps not more so than in previous administrations but probably more effectively. If there is sometimes a disposition for officials to refrain from giving what they believe to be sound advice but which ministers would not like, that tendency – contrary to the popular myth – has always been more to be found than resistance by officials to ministerial policies. If acceptability to ministers has been a factor in some appointments within the Treasury, it seems to me that senior ministers are as entitled as the heads of other organisations to find themselves dealing with people they can get on with, which is something different from appointing people for their politics.

The Treasury today is staffed mainly by career officials who give loyal service to the Conservative government but who gave loyal service to the last Labour government, and who would be equally capable of serving a future Labour (or other alternative) government, if one could get itself elected. But a greater or lesser degree of adjustment is always required in the Treasury, as in most other Departments, after a change of government, and to some extent after the appointment of a different minister under the same government. The adjustment required to the present Conservative government was perhaps more radical than most. It would be outside the scope of this book to attempt to foretell how long it will be before there is a change from a Conservative government, how the civil service will have developed in the meanwhile – for instance, to what extent 'agencies' will catch on – and what degree of adjustment will then be required.

References

CHAPTER 1

Edward Bridges, *The Treasury*, New Whitehall Series no. 12, 1964.
David Willetts, 'The Role of the Prime Minister's Policy Unit' *Public Administration*, vol. 65, no. 4 (winter 1987).

CHAPTER 2

Henry Roseveare, *The Treasury, The Evolution of a British Institution*, Allen Lane, 1969.

CHAPTER 3

William Keegan, *Mrs Thatcher's Economic Experiment*, Allen Lane, 1986.

CHAPTER 4

The Government's Expenditure Plans 1980–81, Cmnd 7746, HMSO, November 1979.
The Government's Expenditure Plans 1980–81 to 1983–84, Cmnd 7841, HMSO, March 1980.
The Next Ten Years: Public Expenditure and Taxation into the 1990s, Cmnd 9189, HMSO, March 1984.
The Government's Expenditure Plans 1987–88 to 1989–90, Cm 56–1, HMSO, January 1987
The Government's Expenditure Plans 1988–89 to 1990–91, Cm 288–1, HMSO, January 1988.
Leo Pliatzky, *Paying and Choosing*, Basil Blackwell, 1985.
Robert Bacon and Walter Eltis, *Britain's Economic Problem: Too Few Producers*, Macmillan, 1976, 1978.

CHAPTER 5

Leo Pliatzky, *Getting and Spending*, Basil Blackwell, 1982; revised edn 1984.

CHAPTER 6

Department of Health and Social Security, *Health Care and its Costs*, HMSO, 1983.

Public Expenditure on the Social Services, Report from the Social Services Committee Session 1986–87, HC413, May 1987.

Science Budget: Allocations 1988–1991, Advisory Board for the Research Councils, December 1987.

A Strategy for Higher Education into the 1990s: The University Grants Commitee's Advice, HMSO, 1984.

CHAPTER 7

A New Public Expenditure Planning Total, Cm 441, HMSO, July 1988.

CHAPTER 8

First Report from the Select Commitee on Procedure (Supply), Session 1980–81, HMSO, July 1981.

Budgetary Reform; Sixth Report from the Treasury and Civil Service Committee, Session 1981–82, HMSO, May 1982.

First Report from the Select Committee on Procedure (Finance), Session 1982–83, HMSO, June 1983.

Financial Reporting to Parliament: Eighth report from the Committee on Public Accounts, Session 1986–87, HMSO, March 1987.

Financial Reporting to Parliament: The Government's Proposals, Cm 375, HMSO, May 1988.

CHAPTER 9

A Framework for Value for Money Audit (available from the National Audit Office).

CHAPTER 10

Anthony Harrison and John Gretton, eds, *Reshaping Central Government*, Policy Journals, 1987.

Improving Management in Government: The Next Steps, HMSO, 1988.

Report on Non-Departmental Public Bodies, Cmnd 7797, HMSO, January 1980.

CHAPTER 11

The Government's Expenditure Plans 1988–89 to 1990–91, Cm 288–1, HMSO, January 1988.

BAA, 1988 Annual Report and Accounts.

British Airways plc, Report and Accounts 1987–88.

British Gas plc, Financial and Operating Statistics 1988.
British Telecom, Report and Accounts 1988: Supplementary Report.

CHAPTER 12
Terence Burns, 'The Government's Financial Strategy, in Eltis and Sindair, eds, *Keynes and Economic Policy: The Relevance of the General Theory After Fifty Years*, Macmillan, forthcoming.
Monetary Control, Cmnd 7858, HMSO, March 1980.
Alan Walters, *Britain's Economic Renaissance: Margaret Thatcher's Reforms 1979–84*, Oxford University Press, 1986.
Denis Healey, *Managing the Economy*, The Russell C. Leffingwell Lectures, Council on Foreign Relations, New York, 1980.
Donald MacDougall, *Don and Mandarin, Memoirs of an Economist* (John Murray 1987)
Nick Gardner, *Decade of Discontent*, Basil Blackwell, 1987.
Financial Statement and Budget Report 1980–81, HMSO, March 1980, and subsequent FSBRs up to March 1983.

CHAPTER 13
Robin Leigh-Pemberton, 'The Instruments of Monetary Policy,' The Seventh Mais Lecture, at the City University Business School, 13 May 1987.
Samuel Brittan, *How to End the 'Monetarist' Controversy*, The Institute of Economic Affairs, 1987.
Financial Statement and Budget Report 1984–85, HMSO, March 1984, and subsequent FSBRs up to March 1987.

CHAPTER 14
Nigel Lawson, *Tax Reform: The Government's Record*, Conservative Political Centre, June 1988.
Financial Statement and Budget Report 1988–89, HMSO, March 1988.

CHAPTER 15
'Her Majesty's Treasury' (Treasury booklet).

Index